THE REAL A...

'Brody Sweeney's superb new book *Making Bread* is full of useful advice for aspiring entrepreneurs and owner-managers looking for good tips about running their business.'

BUSINESS PLUS MAGAZINE

'chirpy and jargon-free'

IRISH INDEPENDENT

'a compulsive 'how-to' book, with lashings of good sense and experience-born wisdom . . . first-class'

BOOKS IRELAND

'*Making Bread* is a terrific entrepreneur's tale. It will galvanise many new entrepreneurs to set out on their journey'

DENIS O'BRIEN, CHAIRMAN, DIGICEL LTD

'A down-to-earth guide compiled in a user-friendly style, full of practical tips to help the young entrepreneur to reach their goals in business'

MARY DAVIS, CEO, SPECIAL OLYMPICS IRELAND

'Brody Sweeney: a man who built one of our most successful franchises but is big enough to admit his mistakes and tell how he learned from them. Read his book.'

TED HARDING, BARRISTER AND FORMER EDITOR,
SUNDAY BUSINESS POST

'Brody Sweeney tells us with total honesty the lessons he has learned the hard way'

DR IVOR KENNY, AUTHOR OF *LEADERS*

'Everybody who runs the course has an interesting and different story to tell. Brody Sweeney is certainly different. His 'new age' way of doing business is very interesting. Read the book.'

LIAM GRIFFIN, FORMER MANAGER, WEXFORD HURLING TEAM

First published in 2005 by Liberties Press
51 Stephens Road | Inchicore | Dublin 8 | Ireland
www.libertiespress.com | info@libertiespress.com
Editorial: +353 (1) 402 0805 | sean@libertiespress.com
Sales and marketing: +353 (1) 453 4363 | peter@libertiespress.com

Trade enquiries to CMD Distribution
55A Spruce Avenue | Stillorgan Industrial Park | Blackrock | County Dublin
Tel: +353 (1) 294 2560
Fax: +353 (1) 294 2564

Copyright Brody Sweeney, 2005

ISBN 0–9545335–8–5

2 4 6 8 10 9 7 5 3

A CIP record for this title is available from the British Library

Cover design by Ros Murphy
Set in Garamond and Stone Sans ITC TT

Printed in Ireland by Colour Books
Unit 105 | Baldoyle Industrial Estate | Dublin 13

Making Bread

The Real Way to Start Up and Stay Up in Business

Brody Sweeney

LIB
ERT
IES

Contents

The Christina Noble
Children's Foundation

Christina Noble is the founder and driving force behind the Christina Noble Children's Foundation. Born into the slums of Dublin, she was to embark on a childhood of pain and betrayal, which included time in an orphanage, living rough in Dublin's Phoenix Park and physical brutality.

In 1989, she founded the Christina Noble Children's Foundation, which is dedicated to helping children in need with education, medical care, social opportunities and job placement in Vietnam and Mongolia.

Since then, the foundation has helped literally tens of thousands of children to live a better life and achieve their potential. For further information on the foundation or to make a donation, please log on to *www.cncf.org*.

Foreword

It was Saturday night in January in Dublin's Mansion House, where the first Dáil met in 1919. The beautiful circular room, with its star-spangled roof, was packed with more than 450 revellers celebrating another great year for the O'Brien's business. A lovely dinner had just been served, and we were about to hold our charity auction. I had gone to change out of my dinner suit into waders and long johns: I was to be auctioned. Well, not me exactly, but rather a day with me, fishing for tuna in the west of Ireland. My friend Jonathan Irwin, who was conducting the auction, was on stage, his voice booming over the microphone. There was a great buzz about the place; in fact, the Mansion House was rocking.

In the toilet, I could hear it all and feel the atmosphere. I paused for a moment: I realised that this was it. This is what I had been working to achieve. The room was full of O'Briens people from all over the world. They were celebrating being part of the O'Briens family – and though the business had been developed by a marvellous team of people, I had started it. This was what I was meant for. It was a beautiful moment. Carpe diem.

Each of us measures our success in different ways. I still get a great sense of achievement from seeing a full car park outside an O'Briens store or standing behind a till, slightly incredulous that people are happy to hand over their hard-earned cash for the privilege of eating and drinking in one of our stores.

O'Briens Irish Sandwich Bars, which was celebrating ten years of franchising that evening, was the company that I had started all those years ago and which had spawned this great gathering. At the time of writing, the business has grown to almost three hundred stores in twelve countries and employs more than three thousand people. It is one of the fastest-growing chains in Europe.

I have mostly enjoyed – and been tremendously proud of – my business experience to date. Running your own business is a marvellous way to develop your talents, and ultimately to fulfil your ambitions and reach your potential.

*

I didn't do well in school academically, despite being educated at one of Ireland's great schools – Blackrock College. I found formal education as I experienced it frustrating and de-motivating. I just wanted to get out into the world and get on with life. I felt as though I had to do a prison sentence in school before I earned my freedom. I still have a natural aversion to textbooks. Those books I do read, I tend to read quickly, and if there's a message there, I try to extract it and use it – if I remember it. This book is not meant to be a textbook. Rather, it is a series of suggested approaches, based on my experience in business, on how to go about starting up or running a small business.

I don't pretend to be an expert on any of the subjects discussed in this book. In fact, my experience of business is limited to what I have gleaned from my time running Prontaprint in Ireland and subsequently O'Briens, as it has grown into an international business.

My experiences are probably similar to those of the many other people who set out to achieve personal fulfilment through owning their own business, and have set up and run such businesses. These experiences are likely to strike a chord with anyone who is thinking of setting up a small business – and to be of interest to people who are already doing so.

Some who read this tome may say: 'I know this Brody Sweeney, and he doesn't do what he says we should do in his book.' Alas, this may be true. I am regrettably not perfect, and have struggled to follow my own lessons; I certainly do not carry them out faultlessly, each and every day. Also, the advice gleaned will not suit every person or every business; the general principles are the things to pick up.

By the way, feel free to dive into any chapter that interests you, rather than feeling that you have to read the book straight through from cover to cover. I hope that, by reading it, you can avoid even one of the mistakes I made – and believe me, I made all the mistakes going, and then some. If this book achieves that much for you, it will have been worth your while reading it – and mine writing it. Finally, embarking on a new business venture is the most stimulating activity you could possibly undertake. Life is for living. Give it a go: what you'll learn from the experience will stand to you for the rest of your life. Good luck.

Brody Sweeney
Dublin, July 2005

1

The Hardest Thing You'll Ever Do

How to cope with the stresses and strains of starting a new enterprise

From the age of fourteen, I thought I wanted to become rich and famous by starting my own business and making a fortune. In truth, I never considered any other type of career. As I matured, I realised that I didn't want to make a lot of money for the sake of it, but rather wanted the freedom to choose how to spend my life. I set a goal that I would be a millionaire by the time I was thirty. At age thirty, I was in debt to the tune of almost €1 million, and tottering on the edge of personal bankruptcy. I set myself a new goal: by the time I was forty I would have earned enough to spend the remainder of my working life (the second half) doing what I wanted to do, and not what I *had* to do. If that meant continuing to run the business, then I would at least have the freedom to choose that option. If it meant taking a step back from the business and trying my hand at writing a book or running for election, I would have the freedom to choose that path instead.

I found the whole experience of attending school frustrating and demotivating, because I viewed the time I spent there as time I could have spent getting a business off the ground and nurturing my ambitions. Even as a child, I was constantly scheming and dreaming, thinking of ways I could become an overnight success. I had no problem visualising my success either: the respect of my peers, money to burn, flash cars, and all the girls begging to be let go out with me!

I started my first real business when I was fifteen years old, during my summer holidays. My father bought a chainsaw to cut down some of the trees around our house. Needless to say, it wasn't long before I was dreaming of setting up a tree-cutting business as the first step on the road to millionaire-hood and fame. So, with Dave Dowling, a friend of mine, I hatched a plan to launch such a business.

Dave's brother Gerry was at the time working for a printing firm, and he printed up some very professional-looking business cards for us. We called our new business 'Vico Enterprises, Tree Surgeons': we though that had a very nice ring to it. With the naivety that comes with youth, we distributed the business cards around very large houses in the Killiney area of south County Dublin where we lived. Completely out of the blue, the owner of one of the houses rang us and asked us to go and see her.

The house was a huge mansion on four acres, with lots of trees that needed attention. Notwithstanding the fact that we were only fifteen years old, we dressed in our best clobber, got some smart-looking notebooks and measuring tapes, and went along to see the lady of the house. We walked around the garden with her, and marked with white paint the trees that needed to be worked on or felled.

Gerry was then called on then to produce a letterhead for us so that we could send an estimate of what the job would cost. Dave and I hummed and hawed over what price we thought we could get away with. When we submitted the price (I think it was £800), we were amazed that the lady of the house accepted it and asked us when we could start! When we had recovered, we arranged a start date and employed both of our elder brothers (which, I have to say, felt very good!) and got stuck into the job.

Everything went well for the first couple of days. On the fourth day, however, things took a turn when we were felling a tree and it fell the wrong way. It almost killed my brother Brian, as it hit the ground very close to where he was standing. The tree fell on top of a wall and ending up lying across the main road, blocking the traffic. We called the fire brigade, who arrived fairly quickly and set about cutting up the tree. At this stage, the police had arrived as well, and uncomfortable questions were being asked about insurance and the legal standing of our company. By the time the fire brigade had removed the tree, there was a half-mile tailback on either side of the road and we were feeling decidedly sheepish. This wasn't helped by the fact that my brother, having recovered from the shock of nearly being killed by the tree, was threatening to kill me!

David and I decided to finish the job as quickly as possible – and then get out of the tree-cutting business. It was far too stressful and dangerous, and anyway, the school holidays were almost over and we had to go back to our mundane lives as students.

*

We all have different motivations when we decide to strike out on our own. For some, the driving force is not having to answer to a boss any more; for others, the attraction is the chance to be in charge of their own destiny. You may want to create something enduring or work together as a couple – or have a passion for something and feel compelled to pursue it. Alternatively, you might want to run a 'lifestyle business' – a business that is in an area that you enjoy and that will provide an income to fund your lifestyle. Finally, a few people may want to conquer the world – or change it.

If you're convinced that going into business on your own is for you, let's have a look at the hard reality of getting started. The points made below are not intended to put you off starting a business but rather to prepare you mentally for what lies ahead of you.

You're the most important element in making the business successful

This seems simple, but a surprising number of people believe that, if the product and the marketing are right, success is bound to follow.

In O'Briens, we talk about the three elements that are required in order to have a successful retail business. These elements are necessary in almost all businesses.

The first is having a good concept. In our case, this means having a range of products that people are willing to buy, at a sufficient margin for our franchisees to make a profit. Very simple – and in our case easy to demonstrate, based on the example of the hundreds of stores that do just that.

Secondly, we need a strong retail location. O'Briens have gained a great deal of experience about what makes a good or bad location for our particular business. While a strong retail location obviously isn't important in a non-retail business, the principle of being easily available to your customers is.

The third, and easily the most important element, is having a good operator to run it. Even if you get the first two elements right, a poor manager will still manage to lose money. Conversely, a great owner can turn a business in a weak location into a success. Recognising that the success or failure of the business is primarily down to you, the entrepreneur, is the first step on the road to business success.

Being passionate about your business is (mostly) not enough

I say 'mostly' because, occasionally, passionate people do get started and make an ongoing success of their businesses primarily as a result of their passion. For the vast majority of people, however, passion alone won't do the trick.

Let me give you an example. Lots of people set up restaurant businesses because they are passionate about food or cooking.

Yet new restaurants have a notoriously high failure rate, and even the top-class ones struggle to make money. To run a successful restaurant, you not only need to prepare and serve great food, you also need a fair amount of expertise in other areas. You need to be good at selecting the right location and negotiating a reasonable deal on the property. You need to be able to prepare and understand a business plan. You need to be a bit of a quantity surveyor, as you work out what it's going to cost to build in the space you have chosen. A talent for design, even if you use an architect, is handy. (Although an architect can design a beautiful building, will anyone want to spend time in it?) Equipment, furniture and raw ingredients have to be sourced, and operating procedures written down, so that levels of consistency can be maintained. Then you have to price the items on the menu, hire staff, train them in, and make sure they work well together as a team. Now you have to put on your marketing and sales hat as you work out how to attract customers and, just as importantly, keep them – and you haven't even opened the doors for business yet!

New start-ups are always difficult

Murphy's Law – whatever can go wrong will go wrong – applies to getting a new business off the ground. Moreover, if you haven't done it before, the project is likely to take twice as long – and cost twice as much – as planned to get it started. With careful planning and management, you can minimise the impact of time and cost, but the frustration – from a wide variety of sources – that new-business owners have to cope with has to be experienced to be believed.

Contrast starting a new job with starting a new business, a mistake quite a few people seem to make. When you show up for work the first day in your new job, you will usually be welcomed, shown around, have things explained to you and be given a fairly clear idea of what you are supposed to do. There will be at least some feeling of order and organisation. If you screw up a little, it doesn't really matter, because it's not your money and it's all part of the 'learning curve'.

New businesses are chaotic. Everything is happening to you for the first time. You are required to make snap decisions, many of which will involve you spending your own money – and often money that you hadn't planned on spending. The unexpected happens all the time, and people let you down; all in all, it can be very difficult to cope. But you know, after a while, things settle down, you start getting used to it, and before long you're ready for your next big challenge.

Keep your head out of the 'coleslaw bucket'

This was a term that we coined in O'Briens for new-business owners who got so caught up in the minutiae of running the business on a day-to-day basis that they forgot about the big picture – like where they were supposed to be going with the business. It's very easy to get bogged down and forget what you're trying to achieve. Even in the smallest business, you are going out on your own for a reason, whether it is to fund a comfortable retirement or pay the mortgage. You need to stand back regularly and look at where you're trying to go.

Most businesses, even those that seem simple to run, are actually fairly complex. We tend to do things we enjoy – and so get stuck into an aspect of the business that isn't particularly important in the grand scheme of things. This approach may be a person's way of dealing with the fact that things are not going exactly as they expected them to.

As a young man, the Dublin chef Conrad Gallagher got so caught up in the PR side of his business that he neglected to make sure that it was making money. Gallagher had what was perceived to be a fantastically successful restaurant in Dublin called Peacock Alley. He was a naturally gifted chef and a larger-than-life character who courted media attention. Flamboyant people such as Gallagher are often not the best business administrators, however. I realised early on that the administrative side of the business wasn't my cup of tea. Initially, rather than doing anything about this, I denied that there was a problem by storing all my financial paperwork in black sacks – out of sight, out of mind, as the saying goes. I eventually realised what a serious situation could develop (I was getting more visits from the sheriff looking to collect late VAT returns than was healthy), and I brought in someone and paid them to keep the books. I regretted that I hadn't done this a long time before and saved myself a lot of heartache.

At O'Briens, we hold regional meeting for all our franchise owners about three or four times a year to help them 'get their heads out of the coleslaw bucket'. For these meetings, they leave the day-to-day affairs of their business lives behind them for a few hours, and we talk about where we are all – franchisor and franchisee – going with the business. The most important aspect of these meetings is the chance they provide for people to meet their colleagues, swap war stories, give out about me, whatever. In most cases, the franchise owners go back to their businesses refreshed and with some new ideas about how to tackle the day-to-day issues that they don't normally get to think about.

Making mistakes is part of the journey towards getting it right

People often ask me at what point O'Briens began to go well. I reply: 'When I ran out of mistakes to make' – about six years after I started. I made every mistake going, from choosing the wrong price points for our sandwiches (our sandwiches were more than twice the price of our nearest competitors when we opened our first store), to making the stores too austere-looking. When we opened our store in Upper Baggot Street in Dublin in 1993, I had the interior fitted out completely in white tiles. At the time, I thought other sandwich bars were dirty, and I wanted to have the cleanest and most hygienic one in town. In fact, I simply managed to make it look like a morgue, and the shop didn't prove very popular with customers. If I have any talent as a businessman, it is a tendency not to make the same mistake twice.

The third-ever O'Briens store to open was in Mary Street on Dublin's north side; the store opened about three years after I had set O'Briens up. I had figured out after opening the first two stores that the number of pedestrians walking past the door of the store was important; what I hadn't figured out at that stage, though, was the importance of the type of people walking past the door. Here we were, having had success selling sandwiches for around £2 on the more wealthy south side of the city, trying to use the same business model on the north side. Unfortunately, the people on Mary Street were looking for three sandwiches for £1! There was no common ground in the middle. The competition was far more experienced than I was, its products were much cheaper than mine, and it killed me. Customers didn't understand what we were about. I had no money to pay for the shop fit: I assumed the cash flow would cover it. My builder was threatening to break my legs because I couldn't pay him. I remember sitting in my van outside the store, with Sinead O'Connor singing her big hit of the time, 'Nothing Compares to You', on the radio. I was crushed by the pressure of trying to keep it all going. I don't think that experience is uncommon among entrepreneurs just starting out.

Five days after opening the shop in Mary Street, I phoned the estate agents and put the property up for sale. Notwithstanding it took a year to sell, and lost money every week it remained in my ownership, if I hadn't made that decision, O'Briens in its entirety would have folded.

In fact, for the first six years of its existence, O'Briens lost money – more money each year than the year before. I used to have a graph on the wall of my office; you know the type – a red line showing an upward trend. People visiting me used to assume that the graph showed the business's sales or profits; I hadn't the heart to tell them that it was the losses.

Running the marathon

I use the analogy of running a marathon to describe what starting a new business is like. Many of those, particularly amateur runners, who have actually run a marathon, describe hitting a 'wall'. Before the event, you prepare by buying new running gear, training hard and psyching yourself up for the challenge ahead. On the starting line, you have an unshakeable belief in your ability to go the distance and be successful. There's excitement in the air: a feeling of camaraderie that comes from taking part in a communal activity, and, on your part, a hunger to get started and put the preparation behind you. The marathon starts, and your energy level is at its peak as you set off.

Most amateur runners start to run into trouble around fifteen or sixteen miles into the race. Your energy level has fallen to zero. Exhaustion sets in, and your legs feel like lead. Worse, you begin to question whether you will be able to finish, and whether you're cut out for marathon running after all. Experienced runners know that this 'wall' is just a passing phase and that, if they can get over it, they can go on to finish the race. In fact, most amateurs do get through the 'wall' and finish, but a small number can't, and give up.

Starting a new business can be a very similar experience. There is the preparation and training before the event; then, on the day of the race, you're excited and nervous but full of confidence. You feel that nothing can hold you back. Even after all the hard work of the final weeks before the race, you have renewed energy for the challenge ahead. Your friends and family are behind you, happy for you, congratulating you on getting this far and wishing you well for the journey ahead. Your new business is shiny and new and yours. You start on a massive high.

Everything goes well for a while. After about two months (the length of time varies) you run into the 'wall'. You become both physically and emotionally exhausted. If you are in the retail business, you will have been standing on a hard stone floor

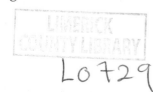

for maybe sixteen hours a day for six days a week – something that people who have been desk workers in a previous life won't have been used to. You will also have been dealing with all the day-to-day hassles that confront any new start-up business. Quite possibly you will have lost weight, and your family will have become a distant memory for you – and will probably feel a bit resentful because you're hardly around any more. Maybe the business isn't going as well as anticipated and the bank manager is putting you under pressure. There are financial pressures at home, and the realisation sinks in that you have no guaranteed pay packet at the end of the week. In short, you feel that this wasn't how things were supposed to be. Some people begin to doubt that they can make a success of their fledgling business and start to lose belief in themselves. In a word, you have hit your low point.

For most of us, such experiences are part of the journey towards running a successful business. Just as the initial high doesn't last, nor does this low patch. You soon begin to see how things can get better, and start to regain your confidence. Only a very few entrepreneurs cannot get through the 'wall'.

The point of including this analogy is to remind you that, if you are prepared for something and know it is likely to happen, you have a much better chance of being able to deal with it.

You need a little luck

I told you about how opening the third O'Briens shop, in Mary Street in Dublin, was a terrible experience, and how I would often sit in my little car van outside the shop, afraid to go in and deal with the mess. I was at a very low ebb then, and lost belief in myself. I had growing responsibilities and a young family on the way, and I was a year behind with the mortgage payments on the house. I was at the tail end of the start-up phase of the business, which I had been managing in an impetuous, seat-of-the-pants, I-know-best kind of way. Instead, I should have been methodical, precise and willing to listen to advice. It was time for me to grow up and take responsibility.

Maybe I just wasn't suited to running my own business. I decided to try and get a salaried job. At the time, Bewley's – Ireland's most famous coffee-house brand, for any non-Irish readers – were advertising for a manager for their Dublin cafés, of which there were four at the time, on Grafton Street, Westmoreland Street, Mary Street and South Great Georges Street. I talked it over with my wife Lulu. We decided that, if I got the job, we would wind O'Briens up. I went for the interview; I didn't get the job. I went home to Lulu that night and declared myself a complete failure. The business was going under and I was unemployable. Looking back on it now, wasn't I lucky that Bewley's never gave me the job?

If you only take three things from this chapter . . .

1   You're the most important element in making the business successful

2   Being passionate about your business is not enough

3   Making mistakes is an important part of getting it right

Most important of all . . .

Keep your head out of the 'coleslaw bucket'

2

Borrowing Money from the Banks

What bank managers really think about your business proposal, and how to handle them

Banks only like lending money to those who don't need it

The relationship with their bank is usually high on the list of perceived problems among new entrepreneurs. We tend to tippy-toe around banks because, in a business sense at least, they have the power of life and death over us. And because they often treat us with disdain but are also one of the keys to the development of a successful business, we are at the same time frightened and enthralled by them.

Most of us learn how to deal with banks through experience. In fact, there are some simple rules and guidelines that can make the whole process of developing a positive relationship with your bank much easier. What follows are some practical stories which you may relate to, followed by some simple tips, which, if applied sensibly, can transform your chances of getting your project funded, while removing much unnecessary hassle and grievance from the process.

*

I had a friend in school whom, to save his blushes, I'll call Fergal. In the years after we left school, Fergal was full of ideas for new business ventures of one sort or another. He would get an idea, quickly figure out how he could turn it into a new business, and in no time at all be off to the bank to get funding for it.

A lot of Fergal's ideas were very creative, but none of them ever seemed to get off the launch pad. Invariably, inadequate or non-existent funding was the main thing holding them back. As Fergal saw it, the banks are the problem. On more than one occasion, he has complained to me: 'They just aren't interested in helping the small businessman. It's an absolute disgrace that, with the profits they're making, they can't support new Irish businesses.'

From where I'm standing, though, it's not the banks that are the problem. Rather, Fergal's approach to the banks is the problem. Try as I might, I can't seem to knock a few simple rules about dealing effectively with banks into his head. And so he just keeps repeating the same mistakes, asking various banks for up to 100 percent funding for this, that or the other business plan. He is genuinely upset when they turn him down every time, and he then gives out endlessly about what a bunch of shysters they are.

Before I set out some tips for dealing with banks, let me tell you about my unethical method of borrowing the crucial seed capital for my first O'Briens store, which opened in South Great Georges Street in Dublin in June 1988. I'm not suggesting that this is a good way to get your business funded: by rights, the fact that I had no capital base in the business should have meant that it was only a matter of time before the business went to the wall.

At the time, I was just winding up my involvement with my last business, Prontaprint. I had got involved with Prontaprint when my father Frank purchased the master franchise rights for the business in the Irish market. I begged him to allow me to drop out of college to run it for him; eventually – and reluctantly – he agreed. I ran the Prontaprint business for eight years, opened sixteen stores and never, ever, turned a profit on it.

When my Dad died in 1988, I decided to sell the business and try to start a new franchise, but after using the cash I received from the sale to pay off creditors, I was broke. All the usual avenues of borrowing from friends and family were closed off for one reason or another. I was desperate to get my business off the ground and knew that, somehow, I had to find a way of manipulating the banking system in order to meet my objective of raising £50,000 to fund the fitting out of my very first O'Briens store, which was to be located on South Great Georges Street in Dublin.

Eventually, I came up with a plan. I approached three different loan companies on the same day and told them that I had just moved into a new flat. Would they lend me £7,000 to furnish it, I asked. Incredibly, because I had approached all of them at the same time and they had therefore been unable to cross-check my loan application with other finance houses, each of the three loan companies lent me the £7,000 without security. Total amount of cash now at my disposal: £21,000.

Sporting my best suit, and armed with an impressive-looking business plan – which a large accounting firm, KPMG, had vetted, and which I had enclosed in a cover bearing their name – and the £21,000 I had raised through my 'furniture loans', I made an appointment to see my bank manager, who was then at Bank of Ireland's College Green branch in Dublin. As I was waiting to see him, I rehearsed my sales pitch: 'I want to start a new sandwich-bar business. Here is my business plan. It will cost £50,000 to execute the plan. I have managed to save £21,000 out of my own resources. Will you lend me the balance of £29,000?'

As I went through the cash-flow projections with the bank's 'relationship manager' (who was in charge of looking after business customers whose surnames began with the letter 'P' to 'Z'), I explained the thinking behind my business plan, and showed him the floor plan of what was to be my first sandwich bar. I could sense that he was impressed. A week later, a letter arrived from Bank of Ireland. Trembling with anticipation, I prised open the envelope. I had been approved for a loan of £29,000!

Incredibly, as a result of using an economical approach to the truth, I now had £50,000 in capital, a well-researched and well-presented business plan – and what I thought was all the experience I needed to set me on the road to business success. As I was to discover, these things were not enough to guarantee that the new business got off to a flying start.

My unorthodox financial strategy was extremely high-risk. In fact, my under-capitalization of the business in the early years – all the initial capital was borrowed – led to years of pain and heartache.

I am not recommending this method of raising seed capital to you or anybody else. In any event, you couldn't get away with it these days, thanks to modern banking technology and efficient credit-checking systems. What my experience showed, however, was that, if you understand the rules under which banks lend money, even a proposal like mine can get funded.

I have set out below some universal truths I have learnt about banking; these truths apply whether you are in Dublin or London, Castlebar or Glasgow. Understanding these things will make your chances of success for your honest proposition much higher than they would otherwise have been.

Banks are run by people

I hear business people saying that this bank or that bank is rubbish, or doesn't understand them, or won't lend them money. But it's not banks that make decisions about your business: it's people – or rather, a person – who decides. So if your manager turns out to be an ogre, or a little Hitler, maybe it's time to change bank managers – not necessarily banks.

As banks are run by people, it's worth trying to develop a relationship with them in the same way you would with anyone else. A bank manager who knows you, who has visited your business, and who understands its highs and lows is more likely to treat you sensitively.

Unfortunately, banks have come up with an ingenious method of ensuring that you don't develop a relationship with your bank manager. In a supreme twist of irony, this method is called the 'relationship manager' system. The thing to remember about relationship managers is that the one thing the bank doesn't want to happen is for you to develop a relationship with them!

All major banks have relationship managers for their business clients. These people are appointed to a particular branch for a relatively short period of time – a deliberate ploy on the part of the bank to make sure that you don't form a relationship with them. The reason for this, apparently, is that if the relationship manager had a real relationship with you – say, for example, that he or she regularly played golf or engaged in some other extra-curricular activity with you – that person would run the risk of making an emotional decision, as opposed to a business one, about lending you money.

It is an irritating but nonetheless inescapable fact of business life that you will invest a lot of time educating your relationship manager about the nuts and bolts and the seasonal highs and lows of your business, only to find that after three years he or she has been moved on, and you have to start the whole process all over again with a new person.

Banks have no interest in taking risks

Essentially, banks lend money only to people who don't need it. The old story about a banker resembling a person who loans you an umbrella on a sunny day and asks you for it back when it starts to rain springs to mind. The key point to bear in mind is that whatever money bank managers have at their disposal will have been deposited by customers, who expect the bank to manage their funds wisely. A customer who deposits his money does not expect the bank to take risks with it by lending it to a risky proposition. And the fact is that a new business is an extremely risky proposition for a bank.

Banks never provide 100 percent funding for commercial business proposals

Although it is true that a bank may provide up to 100 percent funding for certain property-backed business ventures, for normal commercial loans – which most of us use – they do not. If your business plan looks good, and the bank manager likes the 'cut of you', then he or she should have no problem with a 50:50 loan ratio. In other words, for every €100 you put up, the bank will lend you €100. In exceptional circumstances, a bank may lend up to 70 percent of the capital for a start-up businesses (as the bank did for my start-up loan), but a 50 percent loan is normally the maximum level of funding that a bank will sanction.

The logic here is straightforward. From the bank's point of view, the more money you invest in the business yourself, the greater the commitment you are demonstrating to the business, and the less risk there is to the entire business proposition. In addition, the more capital you put in yourself, the less the business has to repay, and so the lower its break-even figure will be.

The point here is that, if you go in to a bank looking for more than 50 percent funding for your new business, and you don't have a track record in business with them, the chances are that you won't succeed.

All banks give their managers authorisation limits

This means that your bank manager will have the authority to lend up to, say, €50,000 without being obliged to refer the matter to an area manager, or whoever.

Your bank manager, whom you will have probably got to know over a number of years, may be happy to take a personal risk with you and lend you €50,000. If you go looking for €60,000, however, you may be pushing the loan application outside the boundaries of his or her decision-making authority. In that case, your bank manager will automatically refer your application to an area manager's office, or to head office, where somebody who has never met you and therefore has no insight into your career history, your ambition or your business idea will make a decision based on cold, hard facts set out on paper. And that decision could be 'no'. Unfortunately, neither you nor your bank manager will be able to do anything to appeal this decision.

Therefore, before approaching any bank for start-up capital, it's worth seeing if you can find out what your bank manager's authorisation limit is. You could try to find out by talking to some existing customers you know who bank at that branch. You could also try asking a friendly staff member, or just be bold and ask the bank manager yourself.

If appropriate (and in a lot of cases it won't be), figure out how you can tailor your business plan so that you are not asking for more money than the bank manager is authorised to lend. Ideally, you should ask for a sum that is just below the authorisation limit, to make everyone feel a little better!

Approach at least three banks at the same time

As a general rule, assuming that you are on reasonably good terms with your own bank manager, you are more likely to get your venture funded by him or her than by a stranger who doesn't know you and with whom you have no track record, even as a personal customer. There are no guarantees, however, that your current bank manager will fund the proposal. Rejection is part and parcel of the whole fund-raising process, as even the most successful entrepreneurs will confirm.

If you are turned down, it might not occur to you, as you nurse your injured pride and survey your broken dreams, that your bank manager might be prejudiced towards certain types of businesses or industries. They may have had their fingers burned by someone in your particular business sector in the past, and therefore be more wary about funding a business in a similar area again.

Some banks may take anything up to six weeks to make a decision. If that decision turns out to be a 'no', then not only have you wasted six valuable weeks, but the rejection may leave you in a bad frame of mind psychologically for your next approach to another banking outfit up the street.

For this reason, it is good business practice to approach a minimum of three banks with the same business plan. If you are lucky enough to receive a positive response from all three, then obviously you should go with the one that gives you the best interest rate, or the best deal – free banking for your first year, or a preferential overdraft rate, for example. Alternatively, you could go back to your own bank with the best terms you received and get them to amend their terms accordingly. In any event, if one or two of the banks turn down your proposal, you won't have wasted weeks or months by approaching them one at a time.

Don't volunteer too much information

A lot of people assume that if you're completely truthful about the take-off potential of your new business, the bank will respect your honesty and respond with support. Unfortunately, however, banks may not want to hear about the realities of your business operating environment – the main reason being that they won't be able to support you if you are too truthful with them.

I remember the signs business that I tried to set up in the early 1980s. The Window Lettering Company, as it was called, did exactly what it said on the tin. I had spotted an opportunity for such a business after ordering signage for our chain of Prontaprint stores, and I and my brother-in-law Kieran O'Sullivan set up the company. I had anticipated that the firm would take four years to turn a profit. Naively, we stated this fact in the business plan that we presented to the bank. This was a mistake. A big mistake. From the bank's point of view, it demonstrated the potential for a high degree of risk and placed a question mark over the repayment capacity of the new business. As a result, our loan application was turned down. After a

31

considerable delay, we eventually persuaded a different bank to provide the funding.

(By the way, the business eventually failed because, with both of us also having full-time jobs, neither of us had the time to run the new company. Lesson: businesses need a dedicated, hands-on manager to set up and run them.)

Have your accountant ring the bank to make an appointment

Don't ask me why this is useful, but I have seen and heard of so many people using it that there must be something in it. By having your accountant call the bank, you are firstly demonstrating a commercial attitude to the bank. Just as importantly, your accountant will be able to ascertain, informally, how your proposal is likely to go down. This may give you a last chance to tweak the plan before making your presentation.

Get the business plan right

Having grasped the basic principles that govern the way banks operate their lending operations, what can you do to improve your chances of getting the money you need? The first weapon in your armoury is the business plan. Here, I strongly recommend that you prepare it yourself. Do not delegate the task to an accountancy firm; the danger is that, if you don't fully understand all the figures in the plan, you may be ill equipped to answer questions in a convincing manner when cross-examined by your bank manager.

With that caveat in mind, it may be a very good idea to present the final document to a leading accountancy firm, with a view to 'bullet-proofing' the numbers, or to seek their endorsement for the stated business proposition. The presence of the logo of one of the big accountancy firms, or a similar heavyweight name, on the cover of the business plan could give your proposal the injection of confidence that is required to impress the bank.

I don't intend to dwell here on the nuts and bolts of writing a business plan, because it is easy to get this information elsewhere. For example, your local library or Chamber of Commerce will have books on this subject, and most major banks provide information packs aimed at start-up operations; these packs set out details of the kind of data that should be contained in a good business plan.

Executive summary

This should be approximately one page (no more than 450 words) in length and should be placed at the beginning of the document. It should comprise a synopsis of the basic business idea, some biographical or career information on you (and your putative business partner or partners) and some details on how the business will be funded, including how much cash you propose to invest yourself.

Believe it or not, some bank managers have admitted to me that they frequently get no further than the executive summary when considering a borrowing request, so do your best to ensure that the text on this page of the plan bristles with conviction and confidence, and makes for compelling reading.

Cash flow

You will need to set out details of projected cash flow for Year One, broken down monthly. For Year Two and Year Three, you need to set out details of quarterly cash flow, while bearing in mind that the projections for these years will be complete pie in the sky! I say 'pie in the sky', because your bank manager will know perfectly well before he or she starts considering your loan request in detail that your business plan does not accurately reflect what is actually going to happen. The only certainty about your business plan is that it will be wrong: you will do better than you think, or worse than you think, but never what your projections say. Bank managers understand this.

All bank managers will have the same view of business plans for new-business start-ups. I remember one of my more friendly bank managers telling me that 'I have never been presented with a business plan in the bank that didn't show the bank being repaid in full, and on time. The reality is that 95 percent of entrepreneurs don't stick to the original terms: they change them, they go bust, or whatever.' For all these reasons, your cash-flow projections and the profit-and-loss account for Year One will be scrutinised most closely, so this is where you should concentrate your efforts.

Be realistic but optimistic

First, in terms of the overall tone and use of language in your business plan, try to make it sound optimistic. Of course, it will need to be based on reality if it is to fly, but it has to be written in such a way that the bank can respond positively to the proposal. In other words, you've got to tell them what they want to hear – without blatantly lying, because there's no mileage in that.

Don't put in too much detail

Lots of us are tempted in our business plans to show off our in-depth knowledge of our areas of expertise. It is not necessarily a good idea to fill the document with statistical data on the industrial sector in which you are proposing to get involved. This type of data rarely impresses. Worse, it may bore the reader witless.

Get your plan critiqued

Before you bring the plan to the bank, show it to a couple of people who know you well, and whose advice you respect. I, for one, have never yet presented a bank manager with my first draft of a business plan. Irrespective of how brilliant I thought the document was, I have always changed it in some way after soliciting the opinions of friends and colleagues.

Practise your meeting with the bank

In the days leading up to your appointment, rehearse your story carefully. Practise your sales pitch. Make sure your presentation takes no longer than thirty minutes. Anticipate some of the awkward questions that might be asked, and prepare your answers to them.

Check your credit rating

It's a good idea to check with your credit bureau what your credit history is like. A credit bureau is an agency used by banks and other financial institutions to check out your credit rating. All the banks which are members of the bureau submit details of your repayment records, which other banks can then view. Customers who have stuck precisely to the original repayment terms for whatever loans they have taken out are given a perfect score. If you have changed your repayment terms, or failed to make some payments on time, you will get a lower score. (In Ireland, the main credit business is called, appropriately enough, the Irish Credit Bureau. Its details are in the phone book.)

If, for example, you had problems with a student loan some years previously, this will be on file somewhere – and will colour the bank's view of you. Remember that, under the Freedom of Information Acts in both Ireland and the UK, you are entitled to contact credit agencies to see what information about you is held on file. If the information is inaccurate, you will have an opportunity to have it corrected and communicated to any banks with which you have dealings.

Manage your ongoing relationship with the bank

Unless you subsequently find an oil well in your back garden, or win the big prize in the Lotto, it is highly unlikely that you will end up seeking just one round of funding during the course of your business career. All banks know that 95 percent of business plans do not predict accurately what will happen. They know that, if things go worse than you had planned, you are likely to want to renegotiate your loan at some point. Banks also hate surprises. For this reason, it's a good idea to keep your manager informed about how the new venture is doing and let him or her know if you are likely to run into cash-flow difficulties before this happens.

You should also invite your bank manager to come and see your new business in operation. Invite him or her to visit the premises, show them around, and try to give them an understanding of what the business is like and how it works. Finally, whenever you pay a visit to the bank manager, bring a small gift – something of low monetary value that features your company logo, a useful office gadget or some product that is associated with your business.

If you only take three things from this chapter . . .

1 People (bank managers) make decisions, not banks

2 Banks never provide 100 percent funding for commercial business proposals

3 Be optimistic but realistic about how much to ask for

Most important of all . . .

Approach three banks at the same time

3

Making an Impression

How to raise your profile and exploit PR and sponsorship to the maximum

Being in business without advertising your presence is like winking in the dark – you know what you're doing, but nobody else does

Like any other aspect of business, raising the profile of the business so that people buy your products is as important as your manufacturing process, or quality control. Yet many of us overlook this fact, or perhaps regard it as being not particularly important. Effective PR says everything about your business. It creates a feeling or emotion in the mind of your consumer, which should create 'positive reinforcement' for your company. Whatever your business – whether it's a small, local one based out of a van, or a bigger entity with global aspirations – there are tried and trusted ways of making the best of your story.

Your story

Telling the story of you, your company, and its particular products or services to the appropriate audience, in a way which conveys what you think is important, is the essence of good PR. Telling that story in a way that doesn't invite cynicism, by for example making unrealistic claims about what your product or service can do, is where it becomes an art form.

It's a fact that, line for line in a newspaper, good editorial on your company is far more credible and effective than paid-for advertising. In O'Briens, we realised this clever fact early on in our development. In fact, it fitted quite neatly with the fact that we had no spare cash to spend on advertising. As a result, we became enthusiastic advocates for PR and it has been the cornerstone of our approach to marketing ever since. So, to get started on this fascinating subject, let's first look at the media.

The media

The media is a collective term for all those channels by which the public pick up their information. Newspapers, both local and national, television, magazines, trade publications and radio are all ways through which you can tell your story to a wide audience.

Conventional wisdom holds that it's hard to get your story written up in the media. Conventional wisdom is wrong. It's certainly difficult to get a poorly written, over-commercial piece written up. Journalists aren't fools, after all. But an intelligent press release, sent to the appropriate journalists and telling your story in an interesting way, is certain to be picked up. This is because it is an inescapable fact of media life that journalists need stories.

Imagine you are the business editor of a national newspaper trying to fill your Saturday column. Sitting there in front of your blank page, you are desperate for stories, particularly if, as often happens in the media, it is a slow news day. There are times when journalists are screaming out for good stories, and if you can come up with an angle, your story could win that coveted space.

While publicly available media are likely to be the main means by which you build your company's story, there are many other things, such as word-of-mouth, public speaking, and your company's behaviour, that influence the public's perception of your company. We will look at these other ways of reaching potential customers later in this chapter.

Building your profile

For many people, particularly owner/managers, or those who dream of running their own business, the thing that people will relate to most with regard to your business is you. So without prostituting yourself, you owe it to yourself to maximise your exposure in an appropriate way, as this will drive customers through your doors.

Think of some of the great personalities who front today's leading businesses. Richard Branson's Virgin is described as a cheeky brand – because Branson comes across as so playful and mischievous. Michael O'Leary, in his drive to reduce flying costs for Ryanair, portrays himself as a champion of the working man.

Anita Roddick has built a reputation for the Body Shop as a defender of the world's poor and marginalized, while Planet Hollywood used its movie-star backers to suggest that, if you dined there, Julia Roberts and George Clooney would be at the next table. All these people garnered thousands of lines of newspaper editorial, acres of pictures, and miles of film to promote their business, for tiny investments relative to the return they would have got from conventional advertising.

Building your profile can be done in very simple ways. Being on your shop floor at your busiest periods. Being your own spokesman. Signing your products. Speaking at local Chambers of Commerce functions about your story. Handling complaints personally. Putting your picture on your products. The important thing is that you are identifying yourself with your product or service; this gives people a more compelling a reason to do business with your company. You should never underestimate the importance of word-of-mouth in building your profile.

Don't forget to think the unthinkable: crisis management

God forbid something really bad happens to your company, but if it did, how would you react? We have tried to think of the really bad things that could happen in O'Briens, and have written a one-page plan as to how to deal with them. Time will tell how robust it is – if it's ever needed – but it's better than nothing, and at least we have taken time to think about how we might react to a problem in an unemotional way, rather than having to think on our feet in the midst of a disaster.

The PR plan

Like any other aspect of your business, PR needs careful planning: a consistent approach is important. I've lost count of the number of people who have said to me: 'PR doesn't work for me. I sent out a press release last month and not a single journalist picked up my story.' This is not surprising, really, as unless the story is absolutely unmissable, nobody will pick up something from an unknown.

We figured out early on that we needed to be consistent. By putting stories in front of journalists on a regular basis, they would eventually get to know the O'Briens name and start writing about us. I was convinced that sending off one piece of literature and sitting back to wait for the calls to come in was a complete waste of time. You needed to build a profile, and this took time and consistency.

So we set up a system whereby we sent out a press release every month. Because we have two audiences in O'Briens – the customers who come into our stores in their thousands to buy our sandwiches and coffee, and the much smaller number who spend hundreds of thousands of euro to buy one of our franchises – we decided we would have two different types of press release.

The first one would be what we called a consumer release; every two months we would send one of these out to all the consumer, health and lifestyle media. This meant that, every other month, we would concentrate on the business-to-business media to raise our profile in the minds of prospective franchise partners.

Speaking of consistency, we have been sending out press releases in this way for more than fifteen years now. And guess what, this approach works. On a few occasions, for short periods, we employed a PR agency, and we still do in our overseas markets, but in truth we didn't need one, as we had a good feel for what to do ourselves, aided of course by our in-house PR guru Elaine Mellon. In Ireland, before we carried out a national TV, radio or press campaign, we had become a national brand, primarily through having a good PR plan that we stuck to. And guess what else: it didn't cost very much!

Should I employ a PR agency?

Some people who run businesses feel that employing a PR agency to carry out their PR plans is the way to go. They may be right. But you should at least consider having a go at it yourself. I can assure you that my ability to write good English is not a proven fact! The reason you should consider doing your PR yourself is that, firstly, when the business is small, it usually can't afford it, and secondly, the story has more authenticity when it doesn't arrive on a PR agent's letterhead.

By compiling a database of journalists, having a plan, and following a few simple tips, sending out regular releases needn't cost you more than the price of the stamps. Even if the releases are not perfect, and even if you don't follow them up with a phone call (although you should), you will be doing infinitely better than the vast majority of businesses, who don't do anything at all.

Getting your press release printed or spoken

Anyone can do this if you think it through properly – although most people don't. For the technical aspects of how to write a press release, you should go to other publications that cover the subject thoroughly – I used a great little book called *Be Your Own PR Man* by Michael Bland – but for the street-smart approach, here are a few tips that have worked well for me:

Keep it to no more than a page

Many of us lose the run of ourselves when talking about our pride and joy. Resist this temptation, and keep your thoughts to well within one A4 sheet.

Write an attention-grabbing headline

The headline '500 IN DUBLIN FOR CONFERENCE' is boring, whereas 'DUBLIN BECOMES WORLD'S SANDWICH CAPITAL FOR WEEKEND' is stronger. Sandwiches per se are not a very interesting story from a PR point of view, unless you make them so. A friend of mine who is a journalist for the *Irish Examiner* told me that, on an average day, the paper receives more than three hundred press releases. He made the point that, if the headline of the piece did not demand attention, it was not even opened. Remember to include the headline in the message title if you are sending the press release by e-mail.

Give the story human and local interest

Readers want to read about people, not products. They may be very interested in what your products can do for people, but not in the products themselves. For example, you may want to write a piece on a new service you're launching. 'O'BRIENS LAUNCH NEW SANDWICH' doesn't quite do it, whereas 'MOYRA DARCY OF DUNDALK BECOMES FIRST IN THE WORLD TO TRY NEW SANDWICH' has much more appeal. Local media in particular want to write about a local angle, or a local boy made good, for example.

Find a funny angle – or any angle

Life's boring enough without adding to it by talking about your company in a boring way. The betting chain Paddy Power uses humour to raise its profile by offering odds on topical events, like giving odds of 100–1 on the Irish rugby international Gordon D'arcy drinking out of a Wavin pipe if Ireland won the Grand Slam in 2005 or, after the death of Pope John Paul II, setting up a stall in St Peter's Square in Rome to take bets on who the new Pope would be. We made great hay out of our Asian MD Hugh Hoyes-Cock winning an award in Singapore for the 'Best British Business in Asian Retailing'. Well, it was funny in Ireland at least!

Write it as if it was an article in a paper

Like most of us, journalists can be a bit lazy, and they may choose to run a piece as it is, rather than going to the trouble of rewriting it. I was surprised initially to see how many of our press releases were reproduced verbatim, with no changes at all.

Don't make it overly commercial

If the piece reads too much like a plug for your product, journalists will not print it and simply give you a free ad. In my opinion, you should avoid putting the name of your service or brand in the headline of the piece, but instead mention it, in context, further on in the article.

Send your releases on a quiet news day or in a particular season

Certain things happen at the same time each year, giving you an opportunity to talk about your business. For example, in September, for most of us it's back to school after the summer break. Most media are writing editorial pieces on the expense of uniforms and books, how to get the older ones to study – and what to put in little Johnny's lunchbox that is healthy and nutritious, and that he won't turn his nose up at. As the nation's sandwich experts, we at O'Briens are eminently qualified to talk about that lunchbox, and we do.

Also, on Mondays, many of the business pages struggle to find news to fill their columns: there is very little business news at the weekend. If you come up with a quirky story or an interesting photo, you can often get something published which otherwise wouldn't make the cut. Think about how you could apply this to your business.

Make it seem as though you're bigger than you really are

Without actually lying, that is. Bigger organisations usually inspire more confidence in the minds of consumers than smaller ones. In the early days of O'Briens, we talked about the number of coffee beans we used each year, which sounded very impressive until you translated that into actual cups of coffee and then into cash – by which time it wasn't very interesting at all.

Sex sells

One of the best PR wheezes we came up with was a sex survey. We got customers around the UK and Ireland to fill out comment cards which asked them their age, sex, favourite sandwich, city of residence and, the killer question, how often a week they made love. Most of the stores had great fun with the survey, although I remember one of our franchise partners in Dublin – Tom Cunningham – getting whacked over the head with a handbag by an older female customer who didn't appreciate being asked that question.

After we'd compiled the results of the survey, we issued releases to both the national and local media, and we had a field day. The national tabloids in the UK and Ireland wrote about our survey extensively, and the local papers picked up the local angle. For example, we sent to the local papers in Leeds in England a press release which showed that a typical O'Briens customer in Leeds liked the chicken-salad sandwich best, and that he or she made love on average 3.2 times per week – a contrast with London, where they only did it 2.1 times.

Using celebrities

As I have a natural aversion to spending good money, we have never paid a celebrity to endorse our products. In truth, it hasn't really been necessary for us.

I have been intrigued recently by the success of the Dove cosmetics ad campaign. They have, on an experimental basis, been using 'real people' to promote their products instead of highly paid and conventionally beautiful movie stars and models. Anecdotally, their sales have gone through the roof.

Giving away freebies

Giveaways can be a great way (if appropriate for your business) of creating goodwill and also getting people to sample your product. We are asked on a regular basis to sponsor races, golf days, walks and other events; this would cost a lot if we were to give actual money. Instead, we offer free water to all the participants, who then hold the bottle for the ten or fifteen minutes it takes to drink it, all the while 'absorbing' our product and thinking about us in, we hope, a positive light.

Guerrilla marketing

I discovered a few years ago that I have been a guerrilla marketeer for years. Guerrilla marketing is a term coined to describe those slightly illegal ways in which some companies promote their products. One of the most famous examples was the band U2 launching their album *Joshua Tree* by playing a free public concert on the roof of a building in Los Angeles. The police went berserk trying to get them to stop, as traffic in the area ground to a standstill. Media all over the world covered the event. It's probably not a coincidence that the album sold quite well.

We used to do the same thing on a much smaller scale in O'Briens. One of the lowest-cost ways of exposing the O'Briens name to many people (other than via our shopfronts, that is) was by hanging banners off bridges and flyovers on busy arterial routes into Dublin. The cost of making a banner was relatively low, compared to the exposure we might receive, so I ordered six of them and in the evenings went out with my brother Greig, who worked alongside me in the early days, building the business, to hang them. I had an idea that hanging banners over public roads was probably illegal, and for good reason: it could be very dangerous if a badly hung banner fell onto fast-moving traffic. But we figured that the worst that could happen was that the banners would be confiscated; indeed, that turned out to be what happened. Notwithstanding that, we got great exposure from using the banners, and no one else in the sandwich business was doing anything like it. One of the attractions for us of trying to market sandwiches was that, at that time, no one else was spending any money on it, so anything we spent was that much more effective.

We suffered the loss of a number of banners, which Dublin Corporation, which had removed them, refused to hand back, saying that we might re-offend. The cost of making new banners began to mount up; sometimes the banners were up for only a matter of hours before they were removed. We soon discovered, however, that most of the Corporation guys didn't work weekends or bank holidays, which meant that, at times of heavy traffic movements, our banners went undisturbed.

We had a long period when we would put the banners up on a Friday evening and remove them again on a Sunday evening. In the intervening period, literally tens of thousands of people were exposed to our logo, at almost no cost. All of this helped fill our stores and popularise our brand.

Many other ideas fall under the term 'guerrilla marketing'. These include sticking leaflets on car windows (again, we didn't know it was illegal), sticking 'footsteps' on the street, leading to a new O'Briens store (curiously, very few local authorities have regulations specifically dealing with this) and handing out free samples of your product at traffic lights.

You are limited only by your imagination, and your capacity to get away with it!

If you only take three things from this chapter . . .

1 Telling your story is the essence of good PR

2 Plan your PR campaign

3 Journalists need stories

Most important of all . . .

You don't need to employ a PR agency to get good PR

4

Selling and Marketing

How to build a brand on a small budget

One of our guiding principles when it comes to the marketing for O'Briens is that the public at large isn't that interested in where – or why – they buy their sandwiches. While I and O'Briens' marketing and sales team sweat and worry about our campaigns, about the new and improved promotions we are launching to help us achieve our objectives, our regular users greet most new innovations with studied indifference.

No matter how hard we try, we can't seem to get people thinking about their lunch before about noon. We've tried everything, but it's no good. In life's great journey, where you buy your sandwiches just isn't up there with love, sex, death, children, where you live, and your career.

In a curious way, acknowledging this has actually been quite helpful for us at O'Briens. We don't expect people to fall over themselves to get into a store to take up the latest special offer, but when, occasionally, they do, we are pleasantly surprised.

We have gone from being sellers to marketers: in other words, we tend not to sell by the traditional direct advertising and sales approach alone, but rather by creating awareness of the brand so that, when someone thinks 'sandwiches', they automatically think 'O'Briens'. The ultimate success of this strategy for us is when you hear someone say they are going for an 'O'Briens' as opposed to going for a sandwich.

Our marketing and sales messages have always been straight and truthful. We have steered well away from the outlandish claims about products that a number of companies make. We try to inject some humour into a normally dull subject, and we tell our story consistently, to as many people as we can make listen.

The beginnings of a brand . . .

The textbooks say that launching a new brand is highly risky and costs millions of pounds in investment. O'Briens, however, has become a brand leader in the sandwich-and-coffee sector in a number of markets without, until recently, ever having had a national campaign on TV, on radio or in the press.

The O'Briens brand name actually came out of a phone book. When I was thinking about setting up the business, I had decided that I wanted it to be big and that we would be going overseas with it.

At the time, back in 1988, Irish culture was quite popular. The Chieftains and U2 were flying the flag musically, *My Left Foot* was playing in the cinemas, and our writers had been doing well for years. In fact, Irishness was perceived to be popular abroad, and I decided to give the new business an Irish theme – somthing to hang our hat on from a marketing point of view.

I figured that, if you put an 'O' in front of a name, it made it Irish, like 'Mac' would imply a Scottish name. I went to the phone book and looked under the 'O' until I came to the most common surname in Ireland: 'O'Brien'. It just seemed right.

While it was always at the back of our minds to become a national brand, we did it 'one store at a time'. In a retail business, easily your most potent marketing tool is your store. It's why you pay such a high rent, compared to, say, renting the same space in an industrial estate. Those twenty feet of shopfront are critical. I remember a seasoned retailing veteran telling me: 'In retailing, your cheapest form of advertising is your lights' – the ones which light up the outside of your store at night.

As we built up our brand, we found that, as we opened more stores, the new stores, instead of cannibalising the business of the existing ones, gave all the stores a lift. Ever more people walked around with a branded cup, or bag, or sandwich and, more recently, water, potato crisps and coffee which they had purchased at one of our stores.

We also recognised early on that most of our customers travelled only a relatively short distance to the store. I remember from some initial market research that we did how upset I was to discover that the No. 1 reason customers shopped with us was not the fact that our sandwiches were amazing or that the stores' interiors were attractive but rather because we were conveniently located. If we were within a short distance of where someone lived or worked, we were fine, but if not, it didn't matter how good we were, people were unlikely to go out of their way to find us.

Our objective became not to be a big national brand but rather, in each store we opened, to make sure we were the brand leader in the area immediately surrounding the store. And it worked.

Be consistent and persistent

I come across many friends in business who say: 'I've produced a magnificent brochure, but it's made no difference.' Or: 'I've done a leaflet drop but gotten no response.' They're usually having trouble getting sales based on their marketing efforts.

With a leaflet drop, we would expect to get a return only after we had been doing drops regularly for six months or so. It can be very discouraging to do a drop and get almost no feedback from it. When money's tight, it's hard to justify spending even more on a method that isn't producing results. For the first two, three or even four drops into the same addresses, the results can be miserable. But after the fifth or sixth, the repetition seems to start to work, and the sales start coming in. It takes nerve and knowledge to hold out until then.

But most people just do one, and then give up because they're not getting the results they want. It's almost a self-fulfilling prophecy.

Use your natural advantages

We all have some natural advantage in our business which we can use to help drive sales. For example, in a retail store, you can leave your lights on at night, create an attractive window display, or draw attention to your store by dressing the outside with balloons, flags or bunting.

When we want to sell our franchises, we have the advantage of being able to display our franchise sales material in our stores. When we want to trial some new products, what better way of doing so than in an existing shop instead of by conducting expensive market research, which may produce questionable results.

In short, think about how you can promote your business in non-obvious ways.

Encourage people to try your product

When we started out in business, one of our problems was people's perception of what our business was actually about. Part of our selling philosophy was to do 'big-portion' products, as a point of difference between us and our competitors. So our chicken sandwich had more fillings than the competitors', had thicker bread, and was more of a meal than a sandwich.

Of course, because it was bigger we had to charge a bit more than our competitors. Unfortunately, many of our prospective customers didn't understand the difference in quality because they had never actually tried the product and only saw the difference in price – the fact that we were dearer.

We understood from this that, if we could get customers to cross the threshold of the store and try a sandwich, even if we had to give it away for almost nothing, we had a fighting chance of getting that customer to come back again.

So we designed our promotions to involve giving away almost-free samples of our products. They were really strong offers, and over time they worked. If we hadn't managed to get people to give us a go, we would never have got the concept going.

Resist mediums that you can't afford or that are wasteful

As soon as your new business start-up becomes common knowledge, you will be plagued with advertising-sales people offering to put your advert on calendars, diaries, local free sheets, radio, TV, supermarket receipts, taxis, match programmes, computer mouse mats, billboards, bus stops and just about anything else that can possibly carry an advertisement. Some of these people are very good at their jobs, and you can find yourself going down a road that is inappropriate, and spending money you can't afford.

It's not that these mediums are bad per se. It's just that it's important to make sure it's right for you. For example, it's unlikely, unless you're a big company, that you could afford to run a TV campaign. If that's the case, you can save time by not meeting people who are selling you advertising space on TV. There may be a great offer to get you an advert in a match programme, but if the match attendees are mostly middle-aged males, it will not be an appropriate place to advertise feminine-hygiene products, for example. When we were developing our new stores armed with the knowledge that most of our customers came from a very short distance around our store and were attracted by the fact that we were conveniently located, we didn't waste time thinking about mediums that didn't address that immediate catchment area. Not only could we not afford to advertise on local radio, but most of the listeners to the radio station were outside the locality, so the bulk of the money we would have spent on radio advertising would have been wasted.

Instead, we found that low-cost advertising methods were the most effective. From handing out balloons outside the stores on a Saturday, to walking around with free samples, to doing direct-mail shots to businesses that were close to us, we hit our target market in a regular and persistent way, and conveniently in ways that were cheaper, relatively, than other methods.

Keep your message simple

There's a great temptation in advertising your company to go into a level of detail that bores the pants off your prospective customers. Adverts are not meant to display your technical knowledge and prowess but rather to explain the benefits of your product from a customer's point of view. Computer adverts are a good example of this in action. I have long since given up trying to understand the terms used in a typical computer advert. I want to know that it will be fast, that it will have adequate memory for my needs, and that the price includes everything. Instead, we get a complete rundown of all the technical features of the computer; my guess is that most people don't understand these features – and don't want to take the trouble to learn about them.

The simplest adverts are often the most effective – think of Prunella Scales in the Tesco ads. (Most of us can find something in Prunella's character – a fussy mother-in-law who is very loyal to Tesco – we can relate to, and so we develop a warm, gooey feeling towards the Tesco brand.) Put yourself in your customer's shoes, think about what they will be looking for from your product, and create an advertisement accordingly. You can either do this yourself – after all, who knows your business and products better than you – or hire the services of an ad agency, where a creative professional may dream up an angle you would never have thought of yourself.

On-brand, off-brand

Have you ever been somewhere that promised you a great time and then let you down? Think of holidays that have gone wrong, claims that were made that covered up penny-pinching (Ryanair's 'You can choose your own seat onboard'), guarantees that were not honoured (Hoover's free-flight fiasco), promises that were not kept ('We'll come back to you tomorrow'). These are examples of companies that are 'off-brand'. In other words, their behaviour is not consistent with the advertising message they put out.

Lulu and I recently had a weekend in Ballymaloe House in Cork, run by the Allen family. We had a great time. It did exactly what it said it would on the tin. Great food served with warm Irish hospitality. What was remarkable about it for me is that such things are difficult to find nowadays.

Is your company's service and quality consistent with what your advertising says? Would you be better off not advertising until you fix a particular problem? These are real questions that you should ask about your business, particularly before you spend money trying to attract more people to your product or service.

Mind your existing customers

Nearly all the customers in a typical O'Briens are regulars. There will be a small number of new people, and some existing customers will drift away, but most are loyalists. Yet we have a terrible habit of treating this group, the lifeblood of the business, with near-indifference when it comes to advertising. In fact, I would go so far as to say that, at times, we alienate them with our advertising for new customers. Have you noticed how companies offering breakdown-recovery services give discounts to new customers, while regular customers who have been loyal to them for years have to pay full price?

Most company's advertising spend is skewed towards getting new customers in instead of trying to hang on to existing customers. Love the customers you have, reward them for their loyalty, tell them they matter, make their interaction with you memorable and warm, treat them as you would want to be treated yourself, and you have a good chance of making sure they keep coming back.

Understand the marketing mix

Making sales is rarely down to one thing alone. There is usually a combination of factors at work. For example, a number of things will influence someone's decision to go ahead and invest the huge sums that are required to open a franchise business.

The franchise brochure will play a small part in this process by creating a first impression of the business. A prospective investor will then probably visit some stores and form an impression of how busy they are and how well-run they appear to be. They will then probably sound out their bank manager, lawyer and accountant and judge their reaction to the proposal. Family and friends will be consulted. A visit to the offices of the franchisor and an interview with the senior management will create a key impression. Finally, our prospective investor will probably talk to some existing franchise partners; this may be the most important piece of the mix so far.

At O'Briens, we made the mistake at the beginning of thinking that it all came down to how beautiful our brochure was, but as you can see, in order of importance this is way down the list.

If you only take three things from this chapter . . .

1 Understand the various elements that make up the marketing mix

2 Resist mediums you can't afford or that are wasteful

3 Encourage people to try your product

Most important of all . . .

Mind your existing customers

5

Suppliers as Friends

How to make suppliers partners in your success

As I grew up in the business world, there was a traditional relationship between customers and suppliers, in which the power of one party (the customer) was used to beat up the other (the supplier). These relationships are still much in evidence in larger, commodity-type businesses like supermarkets, where very powerful customers – the supermarket chains – dictate terms to suppliers to such an extent that a disproportionate amount of the profit on a product ends up in the hands of the retailer. A good example of this is beef production. About 30 percent of the retail price of the beef ends up in the hands of the farmer; this barely covers the costs of his production, never mind allowing him to make a profit on it. In contrast, the retailer enjoys a huge gross margin.

A more modern take on this relationship might be that us customers are completely dependent on our suppliers in order to stay in business. For example, if bread isn't delivered to an O'Briens store in the morning, that store will be out of business. If our suppliers send us food that is off and we unwittingly serve it to a customer, we could be put out of business. If our supplier rips us off so that we can't achieve our margins and make a profit, we could be in big trouble.

Especially in a small business, the traditional approach might alienate the big supplier, so that we can't deal with them. It pays to mind the good suppliers well.

What we want from our suppliers

Now, of course it is a good thing for customers to keep suppliers on their toes, and healthy competition does make businesses more efficient. But for most of us starting out or running a small business, it is usually more valuable to have a strong relationship with suppliers than to spend all our time beating them over the head on price. Price of course becomes more important as you grow into a bigger business, but when you're small it is only one of a range of requirements you have.

As well as the best price, you want the best service and the best quality. We have found that reducing prices can have a knock-on effect on quality. If quality is to be one of the hallmarks of your business, this mightn't be the smartest thing to do.

The other important thing to try to achieve when you're small is to minimise the number of suppliers you have. Keeping a limit on this number has numerous benefits: for instance, you tend to give the suppliers you have larger orders, so they need to earn less per item on whatever they supply to you, and might therefore give you a better price. Fewer suppliers also means less paperwork to work on, fewer deliveries to check in, fewer accounts to reconcile and fewer cheques to write at the end of the month.

What our suppliers want from us

From a supplier's point of view, an ideal customer would be one who bought a predictable but growing range of the supplier's more profitable lines. The goods would be delivered in sufficient quantities so as to make the administration and despatch of the order as efficient as possible, and the goods would be paid for on time.

Unfortunately, from their point of view, there are no ideal customers around, and so they have to accept a compromise.

The extent to which they have to compromise will dictate their view of the relationship, and ultimately whether it's worthwhile for them to work at it.

A great supplier relationship . . .

. . . is one in which both parties co-operate to their mutual advantage and both supplier and customer try to make life easier for each other. For example, we knew some of our larger suppliers had a real headache collecting money from several of our franchise partners. We helped the suppliers institute a system of payment by direct debit. This saved them money on their administration, which they were able to pass on to us in the form of reduced prices. A win-win situation for both parties.

In a great relationship between a company and a supplier, the supplier would feel such a part of 'the family' that he brings in innovations for you. A few of our suppliers are constantly trying to improve the service they provide us with. Derek McDonald of Deemac Coffee in Dublin is one example of this. He's always trying to improve the coffee he sells and understands what we want; at the same time, he tries to drive down the price he gets from his suppliers so that he can pass savings on to us. Derek is shrewd because he can see the long-term benefits to him of this kind of relationship with us. He makes it very difficult for us to part company from him.

Finally, although suppliers should be able to grow with you, in truth most of them either can't or won't. So when you find one that does, hang on to them: they are very valuable.

When you start out as a small business with a big supplier, they are usually in a much stronger position than you to dictate terms. You are an unknown quantity, and your supplier will have seen many small businesses come and go, often getting stung themselves in the process. As your business grows, however, and your supplier gets to know you and your business style, the relationship will become more even.

How to build great relationships
with your suppliers

Communicate your plans and be realistic

If you're in a business which is growing strongly, it will pay you to keep your suppliers up to speed with what you're planning. We have had bitter experience of organising expensive promotions on, say, a satay-chicken sandwich, and then forgetting to inform our suppliers, who promptly ran out of the product as soon as demand for it went above their normal levels. We unreasonably blamed the supplier for not being able to supply while at the same time letting our customers down by stimulating a demand we couldn't meet.

We have also been guilty of giving suppliers pie-in-the-sky predictions of how much of a particular line they might sell. This has meant the supplier being stuck with large amounts of a line that has a short shelf life and which they can't shift. Suppliers have businesses like ours, and they need a realistic assessment of the business they are likely to do in a certain period ahead. It may be that they need to think of putting an extra van on the road, or to increase their manufacturing or warehousing capacity in order to deal with demand.

Change suppliers only after careful consideration

We are inundated all the time with new suppliers trying to get our business who promise the sun, moon and stars. You can't blame a new supplier for trying, but it takes a lot of time to assess them and determine whether there is really any value in switching over to them.

If you're trying to minimise the number of suppliers you have, it's better to compare prices and quality over a basket of products rather than just one. For example, we get small suppliers in trying to sell us, say, a cake they can supply in Dublin but not elsewhere. The cake may be a great product at a great price, but we're not going to set up a new supplier account for just one product, and we're buying for the whole group all around the country. If the product can't be supplied for the same price in Belfast and Cork as it is in Dublin, then it's no good to us. In these cases, if we really like the product we try to introduce the cake manufacturer to one of our distributors, to see if they would consider adding it to the basket of goods they already supply.

Establish specifications

The best way of making sure that you get what you've ordered is to establish specifications for what you're buying. Big companies do this as a matter of course, and there's really no reason why you shouldn't make this part of your purchasing system. A specification for a product would include quality (in a fresh-food product like ham, this could run to the breed of animal to be used, the particular cut of meat, the cooking method and time, the unit delivery weight, the storage temperature and the salt, water and fat content), the delivery method, the packaging to be used and the shelf life.

The trading terms would include the number of deliveries required per day or week, the delivery method, the payment terms, and the invoicing, delivery note or purchase order system to be used. It might also include a complaints procedure and a returns policy.

When all these things are written down, there is much less likelihood of screw-ups caused by one party assuming that the other was doing something that the first party should perhaps have been doing. This also means that, when you are comparing one supplier with another, you are comparing like with like and can then see the real value in a deal.

Offer the carrot of a long-term relationship

Some of our most valuable suppliers, like our Dublin fruit-and-vegetable supplier Noel Murphy, or Keith and Sam in Sam's

Cookies, have been with us since we opened our first store. They have grown their business alongside ours, and we have profited together. Suppliers like to think that they will be doing business with you for a long time, especially if you are growing rapidly.

Assess the relationship every year

While we want to have a relationship of mutual trust and respect with our suppliers, we also want to make sure we're getting good value and that our suppliers are not becoming complacent because the business is coming to them too easily. It is therefore a good idea, on an annual basis, to put the main items you are purchasing out to competitive tender. If you have your specifications written, then this is not a difficult process.

Invite suppliers to co-operate with each other

Inviting co-operation between suppliers can help you in a number of ways. It may not be practical for a small supplier to service a chain of stores around the country, but an existing supplier to the business might be delighted to take on an extra line to add to what he is doing already.

Inviting co-operation can help reduce the number of existing suppliers, while all the suppliers keep their business. There can also be other benefits, such as the packaging suppliers keeping their eyes open for new ways of presenting the cakes for the cake manufacturer, or by swapping war stories on problem customers.

Recognise suppliers' achievements

Our suppliers are no different from the other stakeholders in the business, and they love to be recognised by their peers. We have a small tele-sales company in the UK called Gem Marketing that came up with a completely new way for us to sell catering over the phone. Gem phones prospective customers of our catering service to drum up business. This is a brilliant way of recruiting new customers at a very reasonable cost. Their approach is so successful that it has transformed our catering sales in the stores that have used it. At our annual conference, I got the girl who had set up the company, Jan Everton, to take a bow, and she got a huge cheer. She was very pleased.

You need to be careful that you don't alienate suppliers, however. We have resisted introducing a 'supplier of the year' award as we feel that a company that was trying really hard for us but didn't get the award might feel resentful. Instead, we give awards for long service. By definition, this means that the suppliers must be good: otherwise, we wouldn't continue to do business with them. I know that our long-service awards mean a great deal to our suppliers. They mean a lot to us as well. It's great to catch your suppliers doing something right, just as it is to catch your staff doing the same.

Make them 'part of the family'

We work as hard at keeping our suppliers feeling part of the team as we do at keeping any other players in the business happy. I firmly believe that, if they feel good about their relationship with your company, they will go the extra mile to help you when there is a problem. We invite them out on our socials and to our conferences. We bring them in to show them around the business. We tell them our problems, and they often offer solutions to these problems.

Keep looking for new ones

While it is important to develop your ongoing relationships with your suppliers, it is equally important from a competitive point of view to avoid getting stuck in a rut. With this in mind, you should keep scouring the market for new products and suppliers. Your customers won't forgive you for maintaining the status quo if there are new and improved products available that you have failed to spot.

If you only take three things from this chapter . . .

1 Communicate your plans to your suppliers and be realistic

2 Offer the carrot of a long-term relationship

3 Establish specifications

Most important of all . . .

Change suppliers only after careful consideration

6

Time Is Money

Time-management tips
for those who can't find enough of it

If you want to get a job done, ask a busy person

I don't know who came up with that quote, but it's certainly true. Some people seem to be able to do a million things at once, while others struggle to achieve just one thing at a time.

What is it that these busy people do that enables them to become more effective? Personally, I go through periods of brilliant time management, followed by short periods when I am definitely off the boil and can't seem to achieve anything. I think this is a probably a human trait; many people I know seem to have a similar experience.

I've observed in our own business people like the brothers Bill and Leonard Lynch in Cork, who run more than ten very busy O'Briens stores between them. They never appear to work very hard and always have time to spend with me when I visit, yet their stores are among our very best. Contrast that with a small number of our franchise partners, with only one store, who put in fourteen or fifteen hours a day and wouldn't have time to greet me, never mind sit down with me.

I have to say that the two things that I find to be the greatest time-wasters are going to the toilet and putting petrol in the car. I know, I should get a life! Having said that, some things about time management seem to be universally true:

§   We put off doing things we don't like and spend time doing the things we do like
§   There are never enough hours when we need them most
§   Inevitably, some things in your life get neglected
§   Planning and organisation enable you to achieve more (no rocket science here)

I attended a great course on time management some years ago, run by TMI, Time Manager International, a Danish management consultancy run in Ireland by Conor O'Connell. I say it was great because I still use some of the principles I learnt at it. Here are some of the time-management strategies I learnt from the course, and some other things I've picked up along the way, which I have tried to use in my day-to-day life, and which have undoubtedly helped me to be more efficient and to achieve more.

Contract v. estimate: which are you?

On this course that I attended years ago, one thing has stuck in my mind clearly, and that was the basic definition of people's attitude to time-keeping, where you were either a contract or an estimate person. I am a contract person. If I'm invited out for dinner at 8 PM, I like to arrive at our hosts' door at 8 PM precisely. This means that I will get start getting dressed at 7.15 PM so that we can leave the house in good time at 7.30 PM. My wife Lulu, at least socially, is an estimate person. If she's coming with me to the 8 PM dinner party, she won't hurry. At 8 PM she will decide to go upstairs to get ready. She takes longer than me, so she won't be ready until 8.30. After we leave the house, she will inevitably have forgotten something, and we'll have to go back to the house to get it. We arrive at the party sometime after nine. As we are the complete opposite when it comes to timekeeping, we drive each other bananas. Despite this, I still love her!

It should be noted that Lulu, in her own business dealings, with her company 4giftsdirect.com, turns into a contract person with, apparently, almost no effort at all! 4giftsdirect is a gift delivery and fulfilment business that Lulu started in 1988, the same year as O'Briens, delivering teddy bears on her moped. Since then, it has evolved into a multi-million-euro business and Lulu has at times made me look like a Boy Scout as a businessmen. We've also had four children. She's a busy person. If you need something done, she's the person to ask.

The purpose of this sorry tale is not to share details of my marriage with you but rather to understand that we are all different, and our attitudes to timekeeping are different too. Knowledge is power, so if you look around at the people who work with you, and gauge what type they are, you can organise yourself to deal with it more effectively.

Get some basic organisation

Make a short list of the things that are going on in your life, under broad headings, and refer to them constantly. The idea of this is to remember all the facets of your life and to remind yourself of what they are. I look at this list every week or so and see what needs to be done in each area. In that way, I try to keep on top of things.

My current list is as follows; yours will no doubt be different:

§ family
§ friends
§ business
§ charity
§ personal finances
§ house
§ hobbies
§ politics

Each of the items on the list is then further subdivided. For example, my business section is divided into the following sub-headings, which are subdivided again:

§ people (subdivided into franchisees, customers, suppliers, directors, staff and 'champions' – strong supporters of me in the business, and worth minding)
§ finances
§ business plan
§ marketing and PR
§ product development
§ management
§ communications
§ sponsorships

I keep all this information in a cheap ring binder, with my address book and diary copied from Microsoft Outlook, and a to-do list on the front. I have coloured cardboard dividers – available from any stationers – for each section, to keep things easy to find. That's my low-tech system for keeping an eye on all the things that are going on in my life at any time. It's not very heavy, I can bring it anywhere, and I don't have to plug it in or remember to have spare batteries with me.

Plan your year, month and week

At the start of every year, I set aside an afternoon to sit down and think about what I want to do that year. The O'Briens annual business plan sets out objectives for the various areas of the business for the year ahead, in the context of our rolling five-year plan. The overall plan for the company is communicated to everyone involved in the business so that people understand their role in it and their responsibility for making it happen. Using the annual plan as a guide, and the list above, I think of all the things I will need to do to achieve our objectives. Like me, you will probably have dates that recur every year. Birthdays, annual holidays, exhibitions and trade shows. For me, it is our annual charity cycle and the O'Briens annual conference. These all go into the diary first. Then I think of people I want to meet and try to plan that. Then there are things I would like to do – for example, attend training courses, write this book, run a marathon. I plan and allocate time for each of these objectives. As you see your days beginning to fill up throughout the year, you can begin to look at the more immediate future: the weeks and month ahead. Day-to-day items will always crowd in on your time, but if you have set time aside for your big-picture items, you have that much more chance of achieving them

Spend one day (the same day every week) at your desk

I spend a fair bit of time away from my desk. I try to put Mondays aside in my diary as a day when I will be at my desk, and when my staff and colleagues know I will be there. This gives me a chance to catch up on my paperwork and phone calls, take stock of my priorities (as detailed above), organise the weeks and months ahead, and conduct my regular management meetings with the senior O'Briens staff. The fact that I'm always in the office on Mondays gets me off to a good start and into a routine.

Make 'to do' lists

I live on 'to do' lists. My ring binder has a number of blank sheets at the front for just this purpose. I list all the things that arise during the course of the week, together with things to do from my priorities. I get a great sense of achievement from drawing a line through things when they are done. I forget things so easily that I have to do it this way.

Prioritise

When you get stuck into your to-do list – mine often runs to several pages – you need to have a look at what's important and what can wait. I usually write my list in the order in which I remember to do things – which means that I have all sorts of low-priority and high-priority items mixed together at random. I then separate these items out and write new lists. Remember, important things need attention even if you don't like doing them.

Just do it: get on with the things you don't want to do

Things that you find difficult don't tend to get any easier by you putting them off; in fact, they often become more difficult. I'm no better than most when it comes to this, but about once a week I spend half an hour doing only the things I would prefer not to.

Group together things to do when travelling

Until recently, I was travelling to the UK from my home in Dublin almost every week. In the early days, I used to travel sometimes for only one meeting, which took only an hour. Getting to that meeting involved a four-hour journey there and another four-hour journey home. What a waste of time.

I soon learnt that, by planning my trips a little better, I could make much better use of my time. By thinking of other people I could meet on the trip, I often got four meetings into the one day and saved myself a trip the following week. All the magazines and periodicals I get in work now go onto a 'flight pile', which I take with me when I travel and read on the plane. Airports are also good places to make long phone calls, as you wait in the departure lounge for your flight to be called.

Holding effective meetings

Most business people spend a large amount of their time in meetings of one sort or another. Becoming better at organising and running meetings can represent a real and effective change to your time management and can leave more time available for the more important things. It will also say something about your management style to the people you meet.

Plan for your meetings

The old Irish phrase I was taught as a Boy Scout was 'Bi Ullamh', or 'Be Prepared'. Preparing for meetings is common sense as well as good manners. Reading up on your subject, talking to the people in your business who know most about it and visiting projects under discussion all add up to you having a more constructive meeting. I remember attending a meeting with one of our most important customers, where we were delighted to report a 15 percent increase in like-for-like sales in the customers' outlets. There was a stony silence and our customer announced that their figures showed a 15 percent decline in sales. The meeting was wrecked and I left it feeling sick and embarrassed. It turned out that we had been looking at sales over thirteen four-week periods, whereas the customer had kept their sales records over calendar months. I could easily have noticed this if I had prepared for the meeting properly.

Appoint a chairman

I don't know anyone who hasn't been at a large number of meetings that were a complete waste of time. Meetings that go on too long, where one loud person dominates the agenda, which end up deciding nothing, or, worse, go off in the wrong direction and end up with the wrong decision being made. You can go some way to avoiding this by appointing a chairman for every meeting. Whoever calls the meeting (other than for formal meetings like board meetings) is usually the chairman. Chairman in the informal sense, that is. By that I mean that if, for example, you are making a sales call by appointment with one of your customers, it's up to you to be the chairman – without saying so. It's the chairman's job to:

Set an agenda and time for the meeting, and decide on the outcomes desired

One of the reasons meetings are often a waste of time is that people are not sure why they're there or what decision the meeting is supposed to reach. If you were making a sales call, you might inform your customer in advance: 'I want to see you about our new catering service. I'll only take up fifteen minutes of your time, and if you like what you see, I'd like to give you a free trial.' This is an example of a clear agenda that has a measurable outcome and is time-bound, so your customer knows when he will be free again.

Figure out what you can delegate, and to whom, and then delegate

How often do you find yourself doing something that is really somebody else's job? I know that, in small companies, owners often say to me: 'I have no one to delegate to', but that's not strictly true. For example, when we set up a new O'Briens business with a new franchise partner, they often start out by doing their own paperwork. In the evening, after putting in a hard day's work, and when they're tired and need to relax, they get stuck into an activity that requires a fair amount of brainpower.

The reason given for not getting an accountant to do the books is cost. Yet, when it comes to the business, what price do you place on being tired and lacking the energy to concentrate on the more important stuff? Delegate the paperwork to your accountant, who, if they're any good, will have the discipline to make sure you keep your records up to date, will provide you with management information you can act on, and will leave you free to build sales.

On the positive side, we often forget that delegation is itself another form of training. If you can show someone else how to do it, it relieves you of the monotony of doing the same thing all the time, while teaching a new skill to a colleague.

If you have an ambition to grow your small business into a big business, then you will quickly realise that there's only so much you can do on your own. If you're honest with yourself, you'll know that there are some aspects of the business that you don't enjoy or are not particularly good at. You should, as far you can, plan to delegate these tasks as soon as possible.

Decide who you want to meet

How many times have you left a meeting thinking: 'I didn't need to meet that person.' As with any other aspect of your life, you have to prioritise your meetings so that you don't waste time with people who are not contributing to the achievement of your goals.

Sales people – good ones, that is – can be persistent in forcing you into a meeting you neither need nor want. While I have a great deal of empathy for sales people, who face a difficult job of getting through to people, I also have my business to run. If you have difficulty saying 'no' to people, you should get someone to field your calls for you. As with delegation, maybe someone else in your organisation can handle it.

Make a phone call or go and visit someone instead of sending an e-mail

I know that e-mail is a relatively recent phenomenon in business, and is a great tool in many situations, but it doesn't mean that it needs to replace all human contact entirely. I see many situations in our workplace where e-mail is used but where a phone call would be more appropriate. Often composing and sending the e-mail takes much more time than a conversation would. As we get ever more e-mails arriving on our computers, it is hard to be sure that your message has got through; with a phone call, you at least have some verbal assurance that your message has been heard.

I have a real problem with e-mail in the event of a dispute or argument of any description. Apart from the threat of litigation that comes from putting some disparaging remark in writing, e-mail doesn't pick up tone or inflection. And, as we have seen in our workplace, a rude e-mail can quickly degenerate into a slanging match, if staff don't stop to consider the possible reaction to them letting off steam.

When this new technology front came along, we at O'Briens embraced it with open arms as another way of making communication with our franchise partners easier and more transparent. We quickly had to put a check on this policy, though, and here's why.

One of our franchise partners who was in dispute with us sent me a particularly snotty e-mail which he then copied to all the other franchise partners in our network. Without thinking, I responded to this provocation and copied my indignant reply to all our partners as well.

In no time at all, what had been a relatively minor dispute with one franchisee degenerated into a bad-humoured spat, which created a poor atmosphere among our community. The ease of using e-mail and copying a message to multiple recipients in the main caused the problem, but my poor handling of it only exacerbated the dispute.

We now have a rule that, if a franchise partner has a dispute with us, an e-mail to us is not copied around the network. It was sadly necessary to impose restrictions on the use of e-mail in our business.

If you only take three things from this chapter . . .

1 Are you a contract or an estimate person?

2 Spend a particular day every week at your desk

3 Just do it!

Most important of all . . .

Figure out what you can delegate, and to whom, and then delegate

7

Team Glue

Team-building ideas that work

We all love – and need – to be part of a winning team. Ever since human beings started living in communities, there has been a need for us to be part of, and to identify with, a particular group. These groups are usually headed by a leader – who has either won that position or inherited it.

There is a practical reason why we all love and need to be part of a team: teams are usually more effective than individuals acting on their own. Groups of people inspired or managed (or both) by a great leader can achieve the seemingly impossible, whether it's Ancient Egyptians building the Pyramids, Queen Victoria ruling over a third of the known world, Mahatma Gandhi overturning British rule in India or Neil Armstrong walking on the moon. On a smaller scale, the family unit from the earliest times typically lived longer and ensured that their genes would survive into the future more effectively if they acted as a team.

This situation applies even more so today, as many of our traditional groups have faded away, with the implied loss of identity that this brings. Think of the different groups, headed by a leader, of which we are all part. In Ireland, we are firstly all members of the EU, with its parliament and president, then citizens of Ireland, with an elected Taoiseach. In our working lives, we are usually part of a team (sometimes a very small team) in which we are either a leader or a follower. At home, we have our family team, with its leaders and members. And at play we have our social and sporting teams, with leaders and captains, and members and players.

With all the different teams with which we are involved, have you noticed how you feel differently about each one? Some of the teams we're involved with, like our families, inspire the deepest passions, whereas we are often apathetic or even resentful about others, like the church or the government.

The characteristics of a bad team: the things that turn us off and even make us resentful

I remember the upset caused among friends and family members of my parents' generation, as the Bishop Casey scandal broke some years ago. Bishop Casey was a popular priest, from the west of Ireland, who was fond of the limelight and preached regularly about the sanctity of marriage, the evils of birth outside marriage, and the responsibility of young fathers towards the upbringing of their children. He held himself up as a pragmatic Christian and a practical spiritual leader.

When it was revealed that he had fathered a child and had refused to recognise the child's existence until the child was a teenager, the world seemed to fall in for many older Catholics. For years, there had been a sense of denial among Catholics that there was much wrong with modern Catholicism; the bishops were seen as the last bastion of the traditional Catholic faith. To see an outspoken figurehead of the movement behave in this way was too much for many older Catholics. The hypocrisy of the incident – and it was the hypocrisy that was the problem, not the incident itself (we are all human, after all) – confirmed to a whole generation what it secretly knew but had nevertheless denied.

In this case, the Catholic 'team' – the members and leaders of one of the oldest and most powerful groupings in the country – is still a long way from recovery. The vast majority of its team members, who have been faithful to their Catholic 'family', have been let down by the action of a very few people. The new Pope Benedict XVI, as the leader of the Catholic family, will, I hope, put his own stamp on the Church and rebuild confidence in one of the world's great institutions. Nonetheless, it seems inconceivable now that the organisation will ever again reach the heights of power, influence and effectiveness it enjoyed before.

Why you don't want to lead or be part of a bad team

Teams that perform poorly will probably have some, if not all, of the following features:

A leader or leaders who:

§ is corrupt – materially or morally
§ is ineffective
§ is lazy
§ is disorganised
§ is out of control
§ is conceited or arrogant – blind to criticism
§ surrounds him or herself with 'yes' men and women
§ is out of touch with what his or her members or customers need or want
§ denies that there are problems
§ continues with a course of action even when it is obvious to outsiders that it is doomed

This will translate into a team:

§ that has lost faith and trust in its leaders
§ that doesn't believe in itself
§ in which individual members don't make an effort because they see doing so as pointless
§ that is resigned to losing
§ that becomes introverted and self-serving

§   in which energy is diverted into bitching and back-biting
§   to which outsiders find it difficult to relate
§   that doesn't achieve its goals
§   which individual members don't want to be part of

This is not the sort of team you want if you're trying to set up or run a business. Teams with these characteristics are going nowhere and have no future; change takes place in such teams only when a new leader comes in or the organisation collapses. In the case of the mighty WorldCom, once America's largest utility company, the organisation became so rotten that it eventually fell in on itself. And who would have believed ten years ago that the world's largest accountancy firm, Arthur Andersen, would not exist today?

Create and be part of a great team

So what we want to do, if we can, is to create a great team. Growing a business in a serious way simply isn't possible without building a great team around you: a group of capable people who have a range of skills and personalities and enjoy working hard together to achieve common goals.

Build your team spirit

There's a buzz around great teams that is sometimes almost palpable. It's called 'team spirit' and comes from the very close bond which is created through exceptional leadership and team members stretching themselves personally further than they thought possible. Team spirit is based on an understanding among all the team's members that they can trust each other, that all the members walk the walk rather than merely talking the talk, and that there is a clear vision of where the team is supposed to be going.

Be in charge

All great teams have a leader, not in title but in deed. Great leaders provoke in others negative feelings such as fear and envy and positive feelings like respect, empathy and love. As the team leader, that's what your members will expect from you as they respond in their different ways. Leaders need to be visibly in charge and in control.

You can have a personal relationship with about twenty people

It's no accident that large organisations like the military, police, church or franchises break their large organisations down into sub-groups. This is because large organisations that are centrally focused are nowhere near as successful as smaller, locally managed groups.

I was conscious as we were growing O'Briens that I could have a close relationship with about fifteen to twenty people. By 'close relationship' I mean a situation where I was on first-name terms with someone, could remember their birthday, had a strong interest in their family and friends, and felt I knew them well. Beyond that, it isn't possible to be as close: you are unlikely to experience the same feelings of loyalty and kinship or to know a person well.

This meant that, as the company grew beyond twenty-five employees, I would either have to suffer a loss in the quality of my relationships with my colleagues or delegate some of the people-management aspects of my job. I went down the delegation route. As soon as I was able to do so, I asked my co-director Fiacra Nagle to take over responsibility for about half the people I had previously had working under me, and for him to develop with them the sort of relationship I had tried to maintain with them. He did this – which left me with a lot less than twenty-five people to look after, and the space to build up the number again. In this way, the team could grow to forty people and beyond, and all the team members would have a close working relationship with a leader of the company.

Trust your team

Poor teams have a problem with trust. Great teams accept that 95 percent of people are straight and will, given the right motivation, work hard to achieve their goals.

One of the most common questions I am asked by outsiders is: 'How do you know that your franchisees aren't ripping you off?' I explain that, while we have systems in place to catch defaulters, we run the business for the 95 percent of our franchise partners who are basically honest, not for the 5 percent who think it is smart to rip us off. If we spent all our time trying to catch defaulters, we wouldn't have much time left to develop the positive aspects of a growing business – which is what most of our franchise partners are interested in us doing. We have also learnt that the ones who think it's smart to rip us off aren't actually very smart. Instead of working to improve the sales and margins of their business, they put their energies into something negative; as a result, the business on average doesn't do nearly as well as one that concentrates on the positive.

Delegate responsibility

Contrary to popular belief, team players revel in being given responsibility. Some managers have a tendency to hold on to all the decision-making themselves because, they feel, this is what they are expected to do, or they don't trust their team members. There will always be big decisions that it is your job to take, but there are lots of others where getting involvement from other people will pay dividends.

Let me give you an example. If, in one of our stores, a customer had a problem like having a sandwich with the wrong ingredients delivered to them, in the old days we used to call the manager over to deal with it. By getting the manager involved, an incident which may have been relatively trivial is blown up into something far more dramatic. If the manager was busy doing something else – a very likely scenario, as he or she is the manager, after all – there would also be a possible time delay. Now, we give the front-line staff responsibility to deal with the problem themselves. They have the authority to replace the product, give some free product, or make a refund as appropriate. Most of our staff take this responsibility seriously: they are empowered by having to make a decision for themselves. From our customer's point of view, their problem is generally handled in an efficient, less embarrassing way. Of course, a manager would intervene in the event of a more serious potential problem, such as a health-and-safety inspector commenting on standards of hygiene in a store.

Hire the best people you can afford and weed out the poor performers

Poor performers affect the whole team. One member who doesn't pull their weight means an extra burden for someone else on the team. Some people are just not suited for a particular job, and nothing can change this fact. This is especially true in franchising. One poor franchise operator, who for example doesn't keep their store very clean, affects the perception of the brand, which in turn affects the business of the whole chain. Negative members can drag down the whole team and destroy team spirit for their own narrow motives – for example, if an employee is annoyed with their line manager for some reason, they may then actively invite the other staff to be obstructive or difficult.

In a perfect world, an employee's CV, track record and interview should give you an idea about how that person will perform as an employee. But CVs and interviews are only part of the story. In O'Briens, we had a small number of former McDonalds franchisees apply to us for a franchise. We were very flattered and excited about getting people from arguably the world's best franchise to join us. We hoped that, as McDonald's were known for their superior training and operating systems, this might improve our own business. Alas, in almost every case this did not happen. A person's track record gave no indication as to their future performance. We realised that, in most cases, franchisees don't leave McDonalds – why would they, as it is a lucrative franchise to secure – but are either thrown out or forced out. As a result, we had been dealing not with the cream of their crop but rather with the people they had no future with!

Letting people go is the worst part of my job. We had a period in the mid-1990s when the company was growing strongly but making losses. I found myself having to make the very difficult decision of letting eight people go from our own support-office staff. Eight people whom I had nurtured and made feel part of the team and family. I carried out the 'executions' myself. I had been advised not to give any advance notice, as people sometimes act irrationally and have the capacity to be destructive when they are upset. The shock and bewilderment of the affected people was palpable. It was my lowest day in business. Not dealing with a serious problem with an employee or employees, however, is only storing up problems for later and endangering your work in creating a thriving business.

Balance the personalities

We reached a point a few years ago where I thought we had built up a great team. We were all working hard and having fun: we had a clear vision of the future and a can-do attitude, and were prepared to die for each other. The problem was that we became a bit happy-go-lucky and again weren't making any money.

The problem was that I had drawn together a team with very similar personality traits. We were an outgoing, people-centred bunch, but none of us was particularly interested in figures or the administrative side of the business. The team was seriously out of kilter. Any business needs the type of people we were: people who were good at building relationships, at selling, at team-building. But any serious business also needs the straight, administrative people to support the front end. We identified this problem and took on some new people with the skills the business needed. The change was uncomfortable for the existing managers at the beginning because the newcomers did things a bit differently from us. But it was soon obvious that this had been the correct thing to do: in about six months, it was clear that the skills the new people brought to the organisation complemented those of existing members.

While we're on the subject of personalities, it is important to note that you, as the owner/operator of the business, need to deal with personality conflicts as soon as they arise. In any group, tensions develop from time to time between different members; these tensions, if not dealt with promptly, can become a destructive force in the team.

Be the winner

As we have seen, we all like being part of a winning team. Our team members genuinely believe that we are the best at what we do: that we run the best coffee-and-sandwich chain in Ireland and the UK, that we have the best-run franchise in our markets, and that we are a business leader in terms of putting something back into our communities through our community involvement. We are all proud of these traits, which affect our perception of ourselves. Our people, myself included, have a bit of a swagger because of this. There's a confidence that comes from knowing that you're the best. It's a good feeling. If your company is admired by its peers and is perceived by outsiders as a good place to work, it makes it a much more attractive place to be. It also attracts 'winners' to work with you.

Find out what your company is – or could be – a winner at (we're the world's leading Irish sandwich-bar chain!) and sing it from the rooftops. Make your people feel good about the organisation of which they are part: both their local team and the company as a whole. Create a feeling of exclusivity about the place so that others want to join your team and you become the employer of choice for people seeking a job in your industry.

Team-building tips

Here are a few tips on building a great team:

Let your team know you'll die for them

General George Patton inspired his soldiers before leading them into battle by telling them: 'My principal job is to make sure we all come home together. Alive or dead, we will all be coming home. When we arrive on the battlefield, my feet will be the first to touch the ground, and when we leave the battlefield, mine will be the last feet to leave it: we will leave no one behind.'

I imagine that, if I had been a soldier serving under that general, I would feel confident in my leader and his understanding of my fears and concerns.

A night at the dogs

Taking the team out for a non-curricular evening is a nice way to bond and show that business is not all about making money. Staff meetings like these are a vital way of ensuring that everyone feels part of the team. An evening where you can interact, as opposed to watching a play, for instance, is better. Formal team-building events like war games are very popular. We had a night out dog racing at Shelbourne Park in Dublin recently. It was a great success, as our inexperienced gamblers had a flutter. For a relatively small outlay, we developed a great feeling of camaraderie and goodwill among ourselves, which lasted for months – by which stage it was time to do it again, or something similar.

In the early days of O'Briens, I took the staff out from our then two stores for an evening of ice-skating. There was carnage on the rink, as none of us had ever skated before. The next day, four people rang in sick with bruises and stiffness. So, although a night out is definitely a good idea, I wouldn't recommend ice-skating!

Away weekends

An extension of the night-at-the-dogs idea is for staff to go away for a weekend together. We go for two types of weekend: a social weekend, where we have a team meeting followed by a knees-up, and a team-building weekend like our sponsored cycle ride, where we ostensibly organise a charity fund-raiser, but actually hone our skills as a team in a different field from our day-to-day jobs. Putting on an event like a sponsored cycle involves a real team effort, where the particular work skills of the organisation are used for a non-commercial purpose. For example, in our charity cycle, I head up the fund-raising, Sandra Regan, our purchasing manager, organises the operational support – providing food, water and medical care – Tracey Cusack, our IT manager, the logistics, and Helen Carey, from our accounts team, the budgeting and cash control. We all enjoy doing something different from our day-to-day jobs and revel in putting on a good show on the day.

Training

Nobody does a job in exactly the same way as you would do it yourself, but if you want to grow your business, the first barrier you will reach is your own capacity to be all things to all people. Spending the time training someone in how to do a job properly may well take longer than the time it would take you to do it yourself – the first time. But each time the person does the job after that, you are saving time. Many people leave jobs because the environment in which they are being asked to work is chaotic and they haven't been shown what to do properly. Staff training is particular important for O'Briens and other service-based businesses.

Staff who know their jobs and know their place in the broader organisation are likely to be far more effective – and much more likely to stay – than those who do not. Every member of staff should be given formal induction training into your business and a booklet covering the important points. The O'Briens staff booklet, on top of the practical issues it covers, includes a company history, the philosophy of the business, and a message of welcome from the CEO.

Recognition

We all love getting praise from our peers. I used to be quite cynical about the number of awards ceremonies for various types of businesses there are these days. Having an award for 'Irish Airline of the Year' when there are only three of them struck me as rather pointless and self-serving, but I have realised that, for the people involved, these awards are extremely important. We at O'Briens have an annual conference every year, part of which is an awards ceremony for our franchise partners and suppliers. Each year, I come under pressure from those not directly affected by these awards (i.e. the conference organisers) to shorten the event, because it's quite boring if you're not involved. Those who are involved, though, receive the respect of their peers – the people who are doing the same kind of job as them and know how tough it is to keep the show on the road. This is very important to them.

Praise lavishly, praise your staff in front of others, let them know how proud you are of them, and how proud you are to be part of their team. Recognise everybody involved, not just those on the front line, and watch how good this makes people feel about themselves.

Talk about 'them' and 'us'

I don't mean 'us' being the company and 'them' being the customers. This situation can arise – and can be damaging for a business, particularly one where customer relations are important. I mean 'them' being the competition. *We* are special, unique, better than our competitors; *they* are the bogeymen – out to get us, to put us down, to put us out of business. The enemy. People often get a little more passionate when we talk in these terms, and you can see how bonds are cemented against a perceived threat.

Create systems

Part of our desire to be part of a team is our need for structure and order in our lives. I used to think it funny that, after our babies were born, I sought solace and order in work. In fact, in truth I used to escape from home by going to work every day. Home, with a new baby, meant chaos, disorder, new and surprising events – and exhaustion; work meant, to a large extent, structure and order.

Your staff will want to know what to do, what their part is in the bigger picture and as part of a system which enables them and the rest of the team to work relatively efficiently towards a common goal. You need to create that kind of environment in your workplace. Inducting staff properly, explaining your business objectives, and having written job descriptions are some of the basics of any business.

If you only take three things from this chapter . . .

1 To build a team, you have to trust people

2 Hire the best people you can afford and weed out the poor performers

3 Remember that you can have a personal relationship with about twenty people

Most important of all . . .

Recognise your good performers with a 'thank you' or an award

---

8

Golf Is for Girls

Real ways to network

'Networking' is an overused business term that simply means meeting people who can help you in your business. Over the years, a number of formal 'networking' events or clubs, including trade fairs, conferences, exhibitions and Chambers of Commerce meetings, have come into being – and who hasn't been told of the benefits of networking on the golf course.

But a number of these activities are expensive to participate in and offer scant benefits. What follows is some of my experiences of the good and the bad, and the downright wasteful, in terms of networking. Like most aspects of business covered in this book, good networking isn't complicated; it's the practical application of common sense.

What is networking?

I would define 'networking' as making a conscious effort to meet 'business influencers' relevant to your business. These usually fall under four headings:

1 people you want to sell to
2 people in companies you want to get advice from, or who you want to supply to you

3   people who can introduce you to someone covered in
    (1) and (2) above
4   people in companies you want to 'keep warm' (people
    who may be important for you and your business but
    with whom there is no immediate need to keep in touch)

Planning your networking

At the start of the year, I sit down, with a copy of our business plan and a list of my personal objectives for the year ahead, and spend some time thinking about whom it would be useful for me to meet over the next twelve months. In other words, I formulate a plan of attack.

I try to work out whom, under the headings outlined in the definition above, I want to meet, and when I can meet them. I try to meet a large number of our existing franchise partners (either at meetings or conferences, or by visiting them on a one-to-one basis), as well as a number of suppliers and potential suppliers, who include professional people like bankers and lawyers.

I talk to potential purchasers of our franchise, or indeed consumers of our products in the retail stores, all the time. We keep the O'Briens name in front of this group, either through formal one-to-one meetings (interviews for prospective franchisees, and focus groups for store customers) or through public-speaking engagements at business events – and continue to do so. I think this is as important for other businesses as it is for O'Briens.

People I want to keep warm include our own staff and management team, and business contacts that help us out in various ways throughout the year.

Ways of networking formally

Exhibitions

These are a great way to network. Here's a tip for people who are attending exhibitions: sell to the exhibitor. Although this approach won't make you popular with the exhibitors, with all those potential purchasers in the same room at the same time, it's too tempting to resist! One of our sign manufacturers introduced himself to me in just this way. While I initially gave him short shrift, he was persistent and called back the next day, when I was better disposed to hearing his pitch. (The fact that he had left a brochure with me the first day, which I had read in bed that night, also helped.)

Conferences

My wife Lulu is a conference junkie: she goes to any conference that is relevant to her business. She finds that going away for two or three days, learning from the seminars and meeting different people over breakfast, lunch and dinner allows her to do much more in a few days than she would have been able to do from her desk. In the normal course of events, it would take her months to meet the same number of people, because of the demands of trying to raise four children and keep a model husband happy.

Chamber of Commerce networking events

These events are great for meeting new people, because you don't have to make excuses as to why you're there. Everybody has come for the same reason: to exchange business cards and introduce themselves to a stranger and talk about their business.

Public speaking

This is probably not for everyone: in fact, surveys have shown that many people are more afraid of speaking in public than they are of dying. Event organisers are always looking for speakers who have a local angle. To stand up and tell your story in an honest way, with all the mistakes and bumps in the road thrown in, can make a very compelling case, while at the same time creating empathy and goodwill for your company – and for you personally. I started taking on public-speaking engagements a number of years ago: I reckoned that the audience at these events could be regarded as potential franchise partners or, at the very least, customers for our stores. I found it very difficult at the beginning; in fact, I was a nervous wreck before going on. But it did get easier, and now I mostly enjoy them.

Volunteering for charity fund-raising committees

These can be an excellent way of getting to meet new people in a non-commercial environment. The people on these committees can be generally be categorised as achievers – in other words, exactly the sort of people you would want to network with. Through our work with the Special Olympics World Summer Games in 2003, for instance, I made a whole new set of high-level contacts, some of which have been very helpful to O'Briens and me, both in terms of the business and in relation to my new political career.

Attending charity lunches and balls

My sister Nikki runs an upmarket women's clothes boutique called Havana in Donnybrook, Dublin. She has a great eye and sells beautiful clothes. Her clients, most of whom she knows personally, are from a social grouping who tend to socialise together. Nikki attends and fund-raises for a lot of charity balls and lunches: this gives her the chance to mingle with her customers in an informal setting, while putting something back into the community.

Informal networking on a one-to-one basis

Making an appointment

See the top person

If your target were a company, you should try and see the CEO, or the person in charge of a particular section. Although this is fairly obvious, not many people do it because we don't have the nerve to ask. This person can re-direct you to whoever else in the company may be able to help you, as well as having influence within the organisation.

Ask for advice

Even if you're not really looking for advice, asking for it can lead you into a conversation which can help you sell. So, when phoning to seek an appointment, if you say the reason you want to see the person is to ask him or her for advice, you have a better chance of getting the meeting than if you say you want to sell them something. Most people, even in large companies, like to try and help people, particularly those starting up or running a small business that is trying to break into the big time. Feargal Quinn, the former boss of the Superquinn supermarket chain and a director of the UK supermarket chain Asda, is well-known for giving start-ups in the food sector a break. There are many others just like him in other companies.

Try to see people you think are better than you are

I am reminded of the old adage 'A man is known by the company he keeps.' Networking with the top people in your sector, and not those in the second tier, is undoubtedly a smart thing to do. Other people will respect you for the quality of your contacts, and doors are opened simply by hanging out with people who are influential buyers, sellers or sources of information.

Where to meet

I usually try make it easy for the person who I am meeting, so am prepared to travel to them in order not to inconvenience them. A neutral venue rather than the person's own place of work is probably best: an inexpensive lunch in a local restaurant can be a good idea. I bring people to lunch in one of our O'Briens stores when I can, as I find it a good showcase for the business, and people are as happy to have a light lunch as a heavy one. Busy business people often eat out twice a day, and a light, healthy, non-showy lunch may earn you more brownie points than a heavy, more formal one. Alcohol is almost always a no-no during the day, and in fact may create negative connotations in the mind of your contact.

You've made your appointment . . .

It's a good idea to find out a little bit about whom you are to meet, in order to be better prepared for the meeting. Finding out about someone's interest in horse racing, for example, allows you to drop the subject into the conversation – and make an immediate connection.

It is also a good idea to do a search on the Web by searching for information about them on Google or one of the other Internet search engines. This can often throw up timely information which you can then use to your advantage.

When you actually meet your contact, there are some little tips you can use to elicit information and make the conversation run more smoothly:

Making an impression

For most of us, the best advertisement we have for our businesses is ourselves. We should therefore be ourselves rather than pretending to be someone we're not. I imagine that I'm meeting my wife Lulu's parents for the first time, and think of the impression I want to make on them. They should think that this is someone whom they would like to marry their daughter: handsome, clever, trustworthy and going somewhere! Anyway, you get the idea.

I like to start a business conversation by talking about O'Briens' charity work. This is not to show off how good we are, but it is a neutral subject which shows O'Briens and me in a good light. I might also be able to suss out if my contact has any spare cash to throw into our fund-raising pot!

As we all love to be praised, praise given in a sincere way is almost always well received. When I'm meeting someone for the first time, it's usually someone I think is better than me at something. I use the opportunity of that first meeting to say what that something is.

Ask your contact to introduce you to someone else who may be helpful: this way, your meeting is never wasted, even if the meeting itself doesn't yield much for you directly. If you can, get them to introduce you to the person they mention. An introduction from an influential person is worth its weight in gold.

And the follow-up . . .

Saying 'thank you' to someone for taking time out of their busy schedule to talk to you is only polite, but sadly it has gone out of fashion, along with many of the other social courtesies. I make a point of writing a thank-you card by hand after a meeting. Although I can't prove that this works, I have a feeling that it does. And I'm not talking about an e-mail, a fax or a phone call. A handwritten card or note, saying 'thank you' in a sincere way, shows you are willing to take a bit of time over it.

I send cards and notes often. If I read about someone's success in the papers, or that they have been promoted to a new job – or indeed hear of some problem they've had – I try to send a note or card to let them know I'm thinking of them. At Christmas, I send about five hundred handwritten Christmas cards, with a personal note in each one. I add to this list all the time.

What about golfing and other sports clubs?

Golf – which, incidentally, I don't play – is a great sport, I understand. Out in the open air, in the company of friends, for four or five hours at a stretch, followed by a few drinks at the nineteenth hole, strikes me as a very enjoyable way to spend an afternoon. That doesn't mean it's great for networking, however. Here's why. Yes, you can build your personal relationships on the golf course, and that can be good for business, but the almost unspoken rule about sports-related entertainment is that it's bad form to talk about business directly. By all means have an afternoon off to go to a match or play whichever sport it is you enjoy, with someone you have got to know through business, but be honest about the fact that this is for your own personal enjoyment rather than being a business end in its own right.

Over the course of the year, I am invited to all kinds of corporate days out, many of which I am happy to attend, but I don't feel the need to do business at these events. So feel free to organise your entertainment, and enjoy what's offered to you, but don't include it in your networking goals to any great extent. I have learnt that it would be unwise to rely on this networking method too heavily if you're serious about building your business

Working a room

Before I go to a business gathering, time permitting, I think about who is likely to be there and plan in advance to meet them. Often there will be two, three or even four people whom I would like to meet, and thinking beforehand about meeting them focuses me on achieving that objective. Of course, it is almost certain that someone whom you would like to meet but who you did not know was attending will be there as well, so don't miss the opportunity to introduce yourself to them if it presents itself.

I would then go to the event, check my appearance in the toilet, puff out my chest, make my entrance and seek out my targets. As you may want to meet a number of people, it follows that you won't be able to spend all night with the same person.

So what do you do if you get talking to someone and then can't get away from them? If you're with a colleague, you could have them, by a pre-determined signal, call you away to meet someone else. Alternatively, you could bring the person you're talking to with you to someone else you know, and disentangle yourself from them at that stage. As a last resort, you could bring the person you are talking to with you to meet your target. This is not ideal but is certainly better than not making the connection at all.

Business cards

Business cards are often the only tangible reminder you leave someone with, especially after a casual meeting. They should be very good quality, and should reflect your business. For example, a lawyer would be very unlikely to use a full-colour business card featuring a photo of himself in an open-neck shirt and jeans, whereas this might be a very appropriate style for a hairdresser. Lots of people waste money getting flash business cards done, but this is often a waste of money, when you can least afford it.

Titles on business cards are a bugbear of mine, especially for small companies. Howard Schulz, the CEO of the coffee giant Starbucks, calls himself 'Chief Global Strategist' on his cards. A small bit of an ego problem here, perhaps. Personally, I don't use a title on my cards. That's not a rule, however, as in lots of cases it is necessary to do so.

It's also a good idea to make the cards a bit memorable. I remember years ago getting business cards from Japanese contacts. The cards had Japanese text on one side and the English translation on the other. I thought the cards were really cool. I adapted this idea for us in O'Briens. We put the Irish translation of our cards on the reverse side, which both appeals to our Irish-speaking customers and provides a fun and memorable way for people to remember you. (Try getting someone from England to pronounce the Irish for 'Home of the Sandwich', 'Tintean na gCeaparai'.)

Gifts

I have a true story about gift-giving which I think illustrates the value of giving gifts rather well. Sometimes, when business is going well, unexpectedly nice things can happen. This happened to us a couple of years ago. We were in negotiations with a Saudi Arabian company that was interested in taking a master franchise for O'Briens in the Middle East. The people with whom we were conducting the negotiations were a couple of brothers from a fairly wealthy family. We discussed with them at length the various possibilities for the business in the Middle East, and after a protracted period of time came to a mutually agreed expansion arrangement. Throughout the negotiations, however, I could tell that the brothers were a little nervous about entering into such an arrangement with a small Irish company.

The company's business-development manager, a very nice Palestinian man called Mohammed Hajj, visited us in Dublin with a view to getting the final details of the agreement resolved and the contracts signed. In order to understand a little bit about the Middle East, I had studied some Arabic customs and knew that present-giving was an important part of their culture.

As chance would have it, as part of our fund-raising efforts for the Special Olympics, O'Briens had had some little greetings cards produced. Each card contained a packet of Irish wildflower seeds; the cards were sold through our stores and the profits given to the Special Olympics.

So when Mohammed visited me in Dublin, I sent a hand-painted plate by our friend the ceramic artist Orla Kaminska, as a gift for the Saudi brothers, back with him. As well as the plate, I also sent a hand-written card, which contained one of the little seed packets.

Mohammed returned to Saudi Arabia in due course, and about two weeks later the signed contracts arrived back from the Gulf, with the cheque attached. Apparently, one of the brothers, Saad al-Rasheed, was a keen gardener and had a beautiful farm just outside the Saudi capital Riyadh. When he received our gift, he decided that anyone who would send a greeting card with a packet of seeds as a gift to cement a business deal was exactly the sort of person with whom he would like to do business. In fact, Mohammed later said that the seeds had sealed the deal! That particular incident has shown me that being good in trying to raise money for the Special Olympics helped us get the deal across the line.

If you only take three things from this chapter . . .

1   Try to see people you think are better than you are

2   The best advertisement for the business is you

3   The best networking you can do is also the cheapest

Most important of all . . .

The best way to network is face to face and in person

9

Location, Location, Location

Choosing a winning location
for your business

Our property director in O'Briens, Peter Atkinson, who is a bit of an expert on these things, said to an audience of prospective franchise partners in 1999: 'Of all the aspects of starting a new business, property is the most difficult piece to get right. It is also the most difficult to change if you get it wrong.'

It's relatively simple to change your menu if that's at fault; similarly, personnel can be changed if they're not working out, and an interior can be redecorated. But if the location for the business is fundamentally wrong, it is unlikely to get better over time. Moving location can be extremely expensive to change, and can even bring the business down.

As a retailer, I have been brought up with the mantra of location, location, location. Even so, I have sometimes managed to get things very wrong. The third O'Briens store to open was in Mary Street, in Dublin's north city centre, as I mentioned in Chapter 1. It was in a lovely old Georgian building and had a fireplace on the ground floor. I imagined how things might be in the future, with an open fire set and hordes of shoppers filing through, helping make me a millionaire. In short, I had a gut feeling that this was the right location for me. In this instance, however, my heart ruled my head: my gut feeling was wrong.

Whether you're in retailing to the public or not, location

plays a large part in the decision-making process of any business. So, no matter what business you're in, some of these factors will come into play.

Where you live

Unless you're a complete masochist, you wouldn't take on a business location involving a long commute. If you have found an ideal location, but it's miles from where you live, you could uproot your family, with all that that entails, and relocate. My strong advice on this issue would be not to try to move house and set up a new business at the same. I have seen a number of our franchise partners attempting this: it puts sometimes unbearable pressure on all concerned. (Moving house is reported to be the second most stressful event in a person's life, after the death of a loved one.) Both make enormous demands on your time, and your full energies would be needed for either one.

If you're not willing to relocate, you need to look at potential locations near where you live. This helps you start to narrow down the range of possibilities for your venture, so you don't waste time looking at locations that fall outside your travel range.

Try and take the emotion out of the decision

It's very easy to rationalise a business decision in your own mind by ignoring the unpleasant consequences of it. The Mary Street location I referred to earlier was a case in point. Had I been willing to listen to advice from more seasoned retailers, I would have realised before I even opened the doors there that it was the wrong sort of location for one of our stores.

But I couldn't get the vision of that fireplace out of my mind, and in my mind I blocked out all the negative consequences of setting up there. Although I had no money to pay for the refit, I told myself that the turnover from the new store would be so high that the cash flow from the first two months of trading would be enough to pay the builder. Similarly, although the store was in the wrong part of town for our upmarket clientele, I believed that the fireplace, and the overall look of the store, would draw customers in.

'The day you buy is the day you sell'

I remember hearing this old adage for the first time from Tom Cunningham, who had bought the very first O'Briens franchise from me. He meant that, if you had to sell your premises the day after you bought them, would you get your money back for it. It helps you decide whether you're being too emotional about your purchase and paying too high a price in the first place. He used it as an argument to beat me down on the price he was willing to pay me for the first store he bought from me. This approach helps ground your commercial decision and makes you think about who you would get to take the business from you if you had to get rid of the location in the morning.

Some no-brainers to think about, whatever business you're in

What can you afford?

There's no point considering locations that are outside your budget. Having said that, there is probably an optimal size of location for your type of business. It can be very difficult to get the space, the location and your budget all in sync. In truth, most properties are a compromise: if you can get 80 percent of what you think would be ideal, it is probably worth going ahead with the venture.

Buying versus renting

Often, when trying to secure a location, we think the only option is to rent. But with interest rates at historic lows, it may make little difference to your cash flow to buy instead of rent. Remember, of course, that property speculation is a different business from the one you intend running, and you might be better off sticking to your knitting and not taking the risk!

Planning permission

Will you be able to get planning permission for the type of business you want to operate? Some businesses, like fish-and-chip shops and petrol stations, are notoriously difficult to get planning permission for. A quick telephone call to the planner in the local authority responsible for your area can quickly ascertain whether there are likely to be problems with your proposed venture from a planning point of view.

Where are your customers located?

Trends

What are the trends in the area in which you are proposing to locate? For example, are people moving back into the city centre or will they shop more and more out in the suburbs? Is the area up-and-coming, with new businesses around, or is it in decline, with boarded-up fronts on businesses? All of these factors need to be taken into account.

Are there enough customers in the area, or are they willing to travel? If you set up a business, you cannot afford to be complacent and take the attitude 'If I build it, the customers will come.' If you're in retail, the physical location of your business in relation to where your customers live and work is the most important consideration. If you're in manufacturing, on the other hand, access to skilled workers and raw materials is likely to be a more important factor. If you're in distribution, it might be access to road, rail and air networks. If you're a service provider, you will want to be very close to your customers, but the physical visibility of your building may not play a large part in your business decisions, as you may pick up business in ways other than advertising your presence on a building.

Pull the deal together

When it comes to property transactions, in particular, you should never underestimate the problems associated with getting a deal completed.

Think for a moment about the number of people involved in your new location. Firstly, there's the vendor who is disposing of the property. He may or may not be the ultimate owner (the landlord), who will also have a keen interest in the transaction. Then there's you, trying to acquire the location. Then each party has their own solicitor. Before bringing in architects or town councils, six parties are involved, all of which have different motivations and are moving at different speeds. For example, the person who is disposing of the property may decide that he wants to hang on to the location in order to get the Christmas trade out of it. He doesn't tell you that, though, but instead simply responds very slowly to matters that require his attention.

On the cost side, many entrepreneurs will try to make a project fit their available funds: such wishful thinking often clouds judgements, which need to be precise and realistic. This means that projects end up costing far more than anticipated; this alone can seriously undermine the viability of a new business, to the point where the business may run out of cash before it manages to turn a profit. As part of your business planning, you should talk over your cost estimates with someone you trust but who is not involved with the business. Doing this will give you an unemotional reaction to your estimates.

Destination or impulse?

In retailing, understanding whether your business is a destination store or an impulse store will help you decide where to locate it. IKEA is an example of a destination store: customers will travel literally hundreds of miles solely to visit the store. In fact, there are special sailings for Irish people who want to go to the IKEA in Cardiff, Wales. Although most retailers are destination stores of one kind or another, people are obviously prepared to travel further for a piece of IKEA furniture than they are for a sandwich.

In fact, for sandwich shops and coffee bars, the catchment area could be as small as an area with a 250-yard radius. As a result, there are only a small number of shops, such as IKEA, to which customers are willing to travel a great distance, and far more outlets, such as small post offices, that offer goods or services for which people are prepared to travel only a short distance.

There are few pure impulse stores; examples would include ice-cream shops, shoeshine stands and convenience stores. Impulse goods, by contrast, are fairly common: most retailers include some impulse goods in their product mix. For example, you go to a supermarket to buy bread, toiletries and vegetables, but while you're there, on impulse you buy shampoo, chocolate and a magazine.

Cars or pedestrians

How will customers get to you? In the United States, where downtown areas in most conurbations are very small, the answer would undoubtedly be: by car. As a result, you would want to be in a location that is highly visible, has good access and parking and has a large volume of cars passing each day – and cars filled with the right kind of people for your business. For example, if you are selling luxury cars, you wouldn't want to locate your business in a downmarket area with high unemployment, as very few of the people driving past your business would be able afford your products.

Similar types of retail businesses tend to gather together, either in large, dedicated shopping malls or in industry clusters. For instance, car dealers, furniture and electrical retailers are often found in retail parks, and discount clothing retailers are frequently located in outlet malls.

In Europe, although more and more customers travel by car, large volumes of retail sales are still made in pedestrianised city centres. Many city-centre customers use public transport, and so may not be in a position to carry that wardrobe home on the bus! Home delivery is therefore important for retail business selling bulky items.

The criteria to use when choosing a retail location in an area where the pedestrian is king is much the same as for an area where people get around mainly by car. Some of the factors to consider include the visibility of the site, and the volume of pedestrian traffic past the door at different times of the day. For instance, a business like a sandwich bar, which is primarily a day-time business, will look for a different traffic flow than, say, a video rental store, which is mainly an evening business.

How to find the perfect location

Finding the perfect location takes patience and tenacity. Good properties rarely come on the market, so you need to keep your ear to the ground. The more irons you have in the fire, the better chance you will stand of finding something that suits your needs.

In some cases, we at O'Briens have waited more than eighteen months to find the best location for a store. This may not be practical for the type of business you're in, though.

It's also not a good idea not to give up the day job (if you're starting a new business, that is) until the property has been found and secured. Waiting a long time, with no income coming in, will mean that you will have to dig into your savings to keep the show on the road.

Walk your patch

Get to know the area and keep an eye on businesses that look like they might be closing down. A 'CLOSING DOWN SALE' sign is kind of obvious! See where the peak traffic flows are, and how they change over the course of the day, and between weekdays and weekends. Observe how your competitors are doing.

Put yourself in your potential customer's shoes: as a

customer, where would you want to buy your products? What would the outlet look like? What would make it appealing to you? Is parking important, or is access to public transport a bigger factor in your decision? Do you need to locate your business on the ground floor, or will people come upstairs to you? What about the other businesses in the area: are they smart, and likely to draw customers to you?

Asking these questions helps you start to eliminate unsuitable locations from your list, leaving you with a relatively short list of streets, shopping malls or industrial estates where you can concentrate your energies. An unfocused property search is extremely wasteful of your valuable time.

Meet the main estate agents

If O'Briens were looking for a property in a particular town, we would introduce ourselves to the principal estate agents early on in order to explain our property requirements. Many people think that the job is done by that stage, but of course it's not. Estate agents are like lawyers and accountants: they're not used to chasing after business. So if you plan to sit back and wait for estate agents to contact you with suitable properties, you're going to have a very long wait indeed.

The trick is to introduce yourself to the agents and then keep in touch with them by phone at least once a week. This way, you keep yourself on their radar, and when a suitable location comes up they will think of you.

Tell as many people as you can

You would be surprised at the number of property deals that are made through informal personal contacts. You may well know somebody who knows somebody who is closing down a business or about to put one up for sale. Getting in early before the property officially goes on to the market means that you will be able to discuss terms before the competition is even aware that the property is available.

Keep three or four properties on the boil at the same time

This means that if your first-choice property falls through (which is very likely to happen), you have not wasted two or three months and come to a dead end. The fact that you have alternatives available to you will also enable you to do a better deal on your first-choice property: you will have a fall-back position, if the terms of the deal become unpalatable to you.

Write letters

When all else fails, it's worth getting your estate agent to write to occupiers of attractive properties in the area, to see whether they would be interested in selling a property to you. This is a long shot, but if the estate agent sends out, say, fifty letters, there is a reasonable chance that at least one of the recipients will have plans to move or close their existing premises.

Other location no-brainers

Signage

Ensure that you will get adequate signage for your business. Trying to put a large neon sign for your new fast-food business in a conservation area, while it may well advertise the presence of the business, will be an unhappy and ultimately unsuccessful experience for you.

Do a pedestrian count

If you convert 2 percent of the people walking past your door into customers, you would be doing really well. To assume that you have a good chance of doing more than that would be unrealistic.

Define retail zones

There are instinctive barriers people do not easily cross. For example, people will only reluctantly cross a dual carriageway on foot. Similarly, they won't want to enter a cul-de-sac, or any type of dead end. Also, some locations within a shopping centre are not particularly busy, so watch where crowds congregate.

If you only take three things from this chapter . . .

1 Are you a 'destination' or 'impulse' business

2 'The day you buy is the day you sell'

3 Work out what can you afford to pay, and stick to it

Most important of all . . .

Don't make an emotional decision about where to locate your business

10

Market research

How to carry out effective research without using agencies

'Market research' is really a fancy way of saying 'listening': listening in an intelligent way for the things that are important for your business and that can help you give your customers, or potential customers, what they think they want. Market research is very valuable for the creative brains in your organisation, because it will validate a gut feeling they have – or not validate it, as the case may be. I have been so wrong, so often, in my 'gut feel' for an idea that I have had to discipline myself to research each idea properly until I am certain it is a sure-fire winner.

We all carry out low-level market research all the time, unconsciously. When we try something new on the O'Briens menu, we are conducting practical market research by seeing how our customers react to it. When we change the way we do business in reaction to what our competitors are doing, our informal market research on our competitors is making us react.

Market-research agencies have become an established part of business life. They sprang up in response to the requirements of large companies, which needed to make informed decisions about how to manufacture or market products, before committing large amounts of money and time to them.

Now I don't think there's anything particularly wrong with market-research companies: they have a role to play and are certainly important for large businesses. I just think that, for smaller businesses, you can often get better results by doing your own thing. If you run a small business, or are starting out on your own, and act as your own market-research agency, you may get more realistic results – and will certainly spend far less money – than if you went to one of the blue-chip market-research companies.

For example, when I decided to write this book, and aim it at owners and managers of small- and medium-sized businesses, I tried to put myself in those people's shoes, to determine what they would be interested in reading about.

I came up with thirty chapter headings on subjects that I thought would be of great interest to my target audience. I wrote them on a sheet of paper, with, at the top, the question: 'If you bought this book at an airport, which five chapters would you turn to first?'

Through my own network of contacts, I came up with fifty owners and managers of small businesses, ranging from farmers to lawyers, shopkeepers and restaurateurs. I then – again through personal contacts – got the names of about twenty people who were thinking of starting a new business, or were actually in the process of doing so. I also got a friend of mine who's a lecturer in business at Dublin City University to pass the questionnaire around to thirty of his students.

The questionnaire was sent to almost everybody by e-mail, and I collated all the responses I received. Of the thirty chapter headings, about ten were universally popular. Roughly another five were popular with the owner/managers who were already operating businesses, and a further five proved interesting to those who about to start a business, or to students. Out of this research came the twenty chapters of this book.

This cost me nothing – although I might have to buy a pint for my university friend – and I got meaningful research done. I hope that this research will make the product (the book) more relevant to my target market, and that by extension the sales and profits of the book will be greater than they would have been if I hadn't done the research.

So, depending on the business you're in, here are some other practical ways of conducting market research which won't cost much money and are capable of delivering what your looking for. Before that, though, some warnings about market research:

Be afraid of family and friends

Family and friends usually love you and will therefore want to encourage you – and for that reason may not tell you what they really think about you business idea. Women are great at this. Haven't we all seen girls lying through their teeth over looks? 'You look fantastic in that' might be said to a friend's face, to save her feelings, but when she is talking to another friend about the woman in question, it becomes: 'Did you see the state of her in that dress, it made her look like a hippo!' Friends and work colleagues may also be a little scared of bursting your bubble, and so may tell you only what you want to hear.

Friends and family members often also like to think of themselves as being something of an expert in your business, particularly if it's a business with which they interact. I have discovered in the sandwich and coffee business that we have many thousands of experts among our clientele: that almost all our customers have strong views about how we need to fix the business, or what new products customers are really crying out for. While such comments undoubtedly contain some valid ideas, they are more often just so much waffle from well-intentioned people who don't understand the dynamics of business. You would be well-advised to filter out the good from the bad before you act on any such advice.

Going ahead with a business idea on this basis is risky. You want unbiased, independent and truthful opinions on your business idea from people who don't feel they will be hurting your feelings by giving you a straight answer.

Don't react to the first negative comment you hear

It's very easy to become disheartened by criticism or negative comments, but you should remember that you need to listen to these comments if you are to fine-tune your idea. Let me give you an example. We recently put prices up across our stores in the UK. We had to do this, as our costs were escalating and our margins were therefore weakening. One of our franchisees phoned me up the day after the prices went up. 'You're putting us out of business,' he said. 'All the customers are complaining about our rip-off prices. I had one customer yesterday who spent ten minutes at the till giving me a tongue-lashing over it.'

The penny dropped with me. 'How many people actually complained yesterday?' I asked. 'Um, actually three people,' he said. 'And how many people did you serve yesterday?' I enquired. 'Just over the three hundred mark,' he said, quite proudly. One percent of customers does not translate into 'all the customers'. Our franchisee's reaction was natural, though: he had been embarrassed and remembered the customer who had made a big fuss but had forgotten about – or hadn't paid any attention to - the 99 percent of customers who hadn't commented on the new prices or hadn't noticed them.

I asked the franchisee to hold his prices at the new level for a week, and to ring me back at the end of the week if he still felt that they were too high. I never heard from him on the subject again.

Here are some approaches to carrying out low-level market research yourself:

Focus groups

On the basis that most people are willing to help, you could ask a group of your prospective or existing customers to get together one evening to discuss your product or service and what aspects of it would interest or excite them. A focus group is usually made up of six to eight people, who volunteer their time – anything from an hour right up to a full evening. Sometimes a nominal amount of money, say €50, is given to each participant to cover travel expenses or the inconvenience of attending. You should try to design a questionnaire that will stimulate debate. Devise questions that don't require a 'yes' or 'no' answer. If possible, get a friend or colleague to chair the meeting, and don't identify yourself as the owner/manager, as this may influence what people say about the business.

After you – or your friend or colleague – have asked the question, shut up. The real aim of this exercise is to validate your own opinions on a particular product or service. Is your gut instinct right or wrong? What's wrong with your product? How are customers used to buying the product and, in an ideal world, how would they like to buy it?

You have to be careful to avoid one member of the focus group taking over and to make sure that the quieter members of the group participate. It is also worth keeping an eye on the time so that you get through your agenda. Also, of course, watch out for the 'loyalists': existing customers (who, by definition, think you're good, as they otherwise wouldn't use you) who think you can do no wrong. They may seek to jump to your defence if other members of the group criticise you or your product or service.

Comment cards

In retailing, comment cards are a great, cheap way of capturing customer feedback. We have used them successfully, both actively and passively, since we started. By 'actively', I mean handing them out to customers and asking them to fill them in, whereas using them passively means leaving a pile of them in the store for customers to use as they please.

One of the first times we used a comment card in an active way produced the best market research we ever generated as a company, and all it cost us was the price of printing the cards. In the first few years of O'Briens' existence, we had a fairly clear idea about what we wanted our brand to be: we wanted to offer really good-quality, large-portioned sandwiches and coffee, made to order and served in a friendly Irish environment. A bit like an Irish version of McDonalds, with all disposable plates, cups and cutlery and marketing-led. In fact, leaving aside the disposables, this is still the basis of our brand. Our first serious bit of market research helped us fine-tune this concept and give customers more of what they said they wanted.

I designed the comment cards myself, and sought some key bits of information, including what sex were our customers, how did they get to work, and did they prefer low prices and disposable packaging, or real crockery and higher prices? I then went into five of our stores over lunchtime, and asked about fifty people each time whether they would mind filling out the card for me. In that way, over the course of a week I got a fairly representative sample of the opinions of more than two hundred customers.

The results of the survey were extraordinary. We discovered that the majority of our customers were young, white-collar and female. Yet here we were selling 'Fat City' sandwiches on thick bread, loaded with calories and fat and with no choices for those who wanted a lower-fat offering. We also saw that there was an almost unanimous desire among our customers to be served coffee and sandwiches in real cups and on real plates.

As a result of this survey, we changed our product mix to reflect the tastes of our customers more accurately. We didn't stop selling thick-bread sandwiches, but we did bring on Wrappos™, tossed salads, and low-fat milk for our coffees. We also redesigned the stores to give them a softer, more feminine look. Out went the paper plates and plastic knives and in came real crockery and delft; in order to cover our increased costs, we increased the prices for food and drink that was eaten on the premises. The results proved the point. Sales went up, margins improved and the customers were happier: a real win-win situation for everyone.

Finally, one thing to bear in mind with comment cards is that they are filled out by customers who already use you and who by definition must like your products.

Street surveys

These are carried out in much the same way as the comment-card surveys, except that you usually fill out the questionnaire for the person. The great advantage of this method is that you capture non-customers as well. With people who don't shop with us, the burning question for me is: 'Why are you walking past our store, to buy your food in a competitor's outlet. What are they doing better than us?' We usually carry some free vouchers with us to encourage non-customers to give us a try (brilliantly clever: research and selling mixed together!). As with comment cards, it is best to keep the questions short and to the point, so that you don't end up annoying or taking up too much of the time of your interviewee.

Telephone surveys

Telephone surveys are similar to street surveys except that you phone your customers or prospects instead of getting them to fill out a card. They can be useful if you want to catch people at home in the evening. Telephone surveys also capture people who don't buy from you, and can therefore can give a more real and valid response than a survey carried out exclusively among your loyal customers.

Researching the market by walking about

Of course, nothing actually beats talking to your customers in an informal way, one to one. One-on-one conversations can pick up on questions you never thought of asking, and customers are ideally placed to suggest product improvements, or indeed completely new products.

It's remarkable how often this basic way of listening to

customers is overlooked, particularly in larger organisations. We have a rule in O'Briens that all our support-office staff, including myself, have to spend a day every six months working behind a counter, actually serving customers. I have great difficulty getting everyone to do it, but almost always, when our staff come back from their day in a store, they speak enthusiastically and positively about their experience. This serves a couple of purposes. Firstly, it is a way of keeping the feet of the support-office staff on the ground and helping us understand the practical difficulties of operating a busy store – and, believe me, there are many of them. But it also serves as a way for our staff to hear for themselves what our customers think about us, and our products and service. In particular, I remember some of our marketing team from support office, after spending a day in a store, scrapping a promotion where customers had to fill out an entry form: they found that it just wasn't possible for a customer to do this while standing in a queue.

Market research by trying it out

Sometimes market research isn't enough, or indeed provides the wrong answer, perhaps because the question was asked in the wrong way, or more likely the customer did not know how they would react to the proposed development.

Not long after starting O'Briens, I looked at the possibility of selling a pre-made sandwich. I was conscious that making sandwiches one at a time was offputting for people in a hurry, or who had a large order, as it was quite a slow process. I also had a hunch that some customers didn't really want to interact with staff but just wanted to get in and out of the store with a minimal amount of talking.

This was in my eyes a radical move for us, as our brand at that point had been built on the fact that our sandwiches were made to order, and therefore were fresher than anything you could buy in a newsagent's, petrol station or supermarket. (This was in the days before all these outlets opened their own deli counters.)

We did some limited market research among our existing customers. They said that freshness, and the fact that they could choose their fillings (important if you were on a diet) were the most important reasons why they ate at O'Briens stores. Nonetheless, I wasn't satisfied that we were getting a truthful result.

There was a real fear that introducing a pre-made sandwich could seriously harm the brand, as customers might perceive that we were reducing the quality of the product. I decided that we would try the new sandwich in a couple of stores and see what happened. We had a good result: sales of the pre-made sandwiches took off, and more importantly, sales of our traditional made-to-order sandwiches didn't suffer any decline.

We managed to offer a speedier service for people in a hurry, while introducing a new and profitable revenue source for us. For many of our stores, pre-made sandwiches have become a staple. In fact, we have opened a number of very small, kiosk-type stores that sell only this type of sandwich – and where it would not have been possible, because of the store, to offer made-to-order sandwiches.

Listening to what people are saying as opposed to what you want to hear

Finally, there's a great danger, unless you discipline yourself, that you will only listen to the answers you want to hear. It's human nature to look for answers that reinforce our own thinking and to ignore the ones that don't. I have been my own worst enemy in this, as I ploughed a lonely furrow of self-righteousness, only to be proven wrong, very expensively, in the end.

If enough people who have some knowledge about the subject tell you you're wrong, there's a good chance that they are right, and that your proposal is risky. On the other hand, nothing ventured, nothing gained: many of my entrepreneurial heroes have been people who laughed in the face of conventional wisdom and just did it anyway.

James Dyson, who invented a bagless vacuum clearner that

maintains its suction, was told by countless 'experts' that his business concept would never work. Not only did it work bigtime, but he managed to make his vacuum cleaners sexy – and the fact that they maintained suction important to consumers.

If you only take three things from this chapter . . .

1 When it comes to your business, be afraid of family and friends

2 Don't react to the first negative comment you hear

3 Use focus groups and comment cards

Most important of all . . .

Listen to what people say as opposed to what you want to hear

11

Pearls of Wisdom

Words of advice
from the great and the good

I love to meet people I admire, or indeed read about famous people and pick up some pearl of wisdom from their experiences. What follows, in no particular order, are some of the best bits of advice given to me, as well as my favourite sayings or quotations, and why I like them.

> *Don't worry about how much you think the other guy is making –*
> *concentrate on your own business*
>
> EDWIN THIRLWELL, founder of the Prontaprint quick-print chain

This always struck me as great advice, because my natural reaction to people around me who appeared to be performing better than me was to spend my time and energy speculating as to what was the secret to their business success.

A good example of this was during the recent dot-com boom. It was an incredibly frustrating time if you were not one of those blessed with their own dot-com company. At the time, I had been about eight years running my own business, at that stage with some success. Yet everyone around me seemed to be dreaming up dot-com projects and transforming their companies into overnight successes.

I decided to come up with a dot-com angle for O'Briens, and we did. We designed our website so that you could order sandwiches online. It was a very sophisticated piece of software that did exactly what it said on the tin. Unfortunately, no one ordered from it, and after a respectable period of time had elapsed, we took it down.

All around me, companies were getting caught up in the frenzy. The high-street electrical retailer Dixons got it spectacularly right and made a fortune for its shareholders with its Freeserve site. (Freeserve was one of the first Internet-portal sites; they built up their customer numbers very quickly by preloading their own software on all the computers they sold through their Dixons stores.) Fyffes, one of Europe's largest fruit importers, got it spectacularly wrong after they shut their 'world of fruit' site and their share price collapsed – something from which they have taken a long time to recover. Companies like the IT start-up Baltimore Technologies became completely caught up in the hype and went from virtually nothing to FTSE 100 operations overnight, before they went down in flames.

I think we were lucky in O'Briens. We got mildly distracted for a while by the dot-com bubble but didn't spend huge effort or money changing our strategy. Instead, we reaffirmed our own reason for being, forgot about how much money we thought other people were making, and concentrated on selling good sandwiches and coffee – which was, after all, the reason we had come into being.

Many of life's failures are people who did not realize how close they were to success when they gave up

THOMAS EDISON

Because of my work with, firstly, Prontaprint and secondly, O'Briens – both of them franchise businesses – I have observed literally hundreds of different people setting up in business for the first time. You would expect that people who were given the same training and the same brand name to trade under, with the same range of products, sold at the same price, would all get on pretty much the same.

You would be very wrong. In my experience, the principal determinant of the success or failure of a business is the person who is driving that business. A person's level of belief in themselves, their perseverance and their determination to overcome the many obstacles in their way sorts the men from the boys – and the women from the girls!

One of my franchise partners, Ed, described setting up his new business as follows: 'I was exhausted. Since the business opened, I hade been working sixteen-hour days, six days a week. I felt I had a day off on Sundays because I only worked eight hours! I haven't seen anything of my wife and family. The over-run on building the store coincided with sales being slower than expected, and my bank manager started to put me under pressure. The level of detail had overwhelmed me, and I felt I couldn't go on. I wanted to give up. It was too much for me.'

I explained to Ed that what he was going through was part of his journey to business success. Success was just over the hill; he could nearly touch it; he should just persevere a little longer. For Ed, it did come right, and he now has a successful business. Others, unfortunately, didn't realize how close they were to achieving their dream and were not successful.

The secret of success is to do the common things uncommonly well

JOHN D. ROCKEFELLER

Rockefeller, the commercial prince of American business, understood very well what most of us take years to find out: most good businesses are based on very simple concepts that are excellently executed.

Michael O'Leary in Ryanair is uncommonly good at reducing

costs in order to offer consumers the cheapest airfares. Ray Kroc of McDonalds became uncommonly good at serving hamburgers and fries cleanly, consistently and profitably. The Google search engine became the biggest in the world because the company's founders took a common Internet tool – the search engine – and made it uncommonly easy to use.

The O'Briens business concept is simple: to sell really high-quality sandwiches and coffee. Not the flashest sandwiches in town (as fewer people will want to buy them, they will have a limited market), but if we do a cheese sandwich, I want it to be the best cheese sandwich on the street. Before we came along, businesses had been selling cheese sandwiches for many years. These businesses had two things in common: the quality and accessibility of the sandwiches was not very good, and it was very hard to make money from selling them.

So, taking Rockefeller at his word, we did what we had to do to the humble cheese sandwich. Even though we hadn't heard of Rockefeller then, we instinctively did the right things: we concentrated on doing the little things right. We made the sandwich bigger (the evolution of our thick-bread sandwich!) and, by having it prepared to order, fresher. We branded it so that you identified this bigger, fresher sandwich with O'Briens. We were smarter with our marketing, allowing people to sample it for free. We charged enough to allow us to make a small profit, so that we could re-invest in product development and attractive packaging. We opened more stores in more convenient locations, enabling more people to try the product. It's hard for people to realise now that doing these simple things to the basic cheese sandwich allowed us to create a whole new industry sector where none had existed before.

Keep away from people who try and belittle your ambitions. Small people always do that, but the really great ones make you feel that you, too, can become great.

MARK TWAIN

We all have acquaintances that fall into the doom-and-gloom category. Those eternal pessimists who see black where you see white and who always fear the worst; given sufficient time, you just might start to listen to them. As a result, it can be very dangerous to associate with them at the outset of a new venture.

Most of us also have friends and acquaintances who are positive about life and love, and who are usually willing to see the positive side of a situation. The old adage 'a man is known by the company he keeps' comes to mind. Most of us love to be with someone who pushes the boundaries of what's possible and encourages us to give something a go.

Starting or running a small business requires extraordinary optimism. To begin with, the fact that no one else has done your particular venture, in the specific way that you are going about it, means that it's untried. Untried things are dangerous. They carry a high risk of going wrong. It might fail, and you could lose everything. Yet those of us who have taken the plunge accepted these impediments and just got on with it.

Even after we have got going in the venture, we're not out of the woods. Although we might have made our mind up at the outset that we should pursue a particular line, we are susceptible, under sustained pressure, to changing our minds and becoming scared that our original plans either can't or won't work. In other words, negative people can make you lose confidence in yourself. You may also be conscious that friends and colleagues are a little jealous of your perceived success and feel that you need to be brought down a peg or too.

For any argument you might care to put up, there will always be an opposing view. And as Irish readers will know, we Irish have opinions on everything. If I believe in something, I try to listen to opposing views (but am not always successful in this!). Bitter experience has taught me that there will always be naysayers and knockers who feel that they have to tell you how difficult and risky your proposed action is, and to warn you of your folly.

Give the negative people in your life a wide berth, or they will drag you down with them. I have made it a rule to surround myself with positive people as far as possible. I am sure that this helps contribute to a more positive life, as I don't tend to dwell on the negative aspect of any situation for too long.

Never interfere with the enemy when he is making a mistake

Sun Tzu, in *The Art of War*

I couldn't understand why our closest competitor in the coffee business in Ireland, Bewley's Cafés, never came after the cappuccino-to-go market in the same way that we did. Back in the 1990s, we discovered a little company based in Seattle in America's Northwest, called Starbucks. The were setting the coffee-shop market on fire, selling espresso-based coffee drinks for people to take away in paper cups with domed lids.

I visited Seattle with my friend and colleague Stephen Knight; every street corner appeared to have its own Starbucks. People were walking along drinking from these paper cups with the funny lids, and we immediately realised the potential of this approach for Ireland and the UK.

Back in Ireland, we immediately got rid of our old coffee machines and replaced them with the latest Gaggia espresso machines from Italy. These machines, together with our newly printed paper cups and domed lids, gave us a head start in Ireland's burgeoning coffee culture. It was a very sweet business to get into. Our 'old' coffee, brewed in big pots and sold in polystyrene cups, was not a great seller, accounting for only a fraction of sales.

We brought in our own espresso-based coffee, served in

paper cups, and increased the retail price substantially. We couldn't make enough of it to keep up with demand, and coffee went from being a sideshow in our business to the company's No. 2-selling product.

We opened more and more stores, all the time looking over our shoulders to see how Bewley's would respond. Apart from having lots of stores selling the new-style coffees, we did nothing to draw attention to ourselves and so possibly alert Bewley's and other competitors to the opportunity they were missing. Before long, we were selling more coffee on the high street than any other chain, and the gap between us and everyone else just got bigger – as it continues to be to this day.

Bewley's made a mistake by not making this new coffee market their own, and we weren't going to help them by advertising the fact. It was a good example of Sun Tzu's advice in action. Incidentally, Paddy Campbell, the man who rescued Bewley's as it was about to go bust, is an entrepreneur I have the height of respect for. He took on Bewley's when none of the rest of us had the nerve to touch it.

Equity is blood

MICHAEL SMURFIT, FORMER CEO OF THE SMURFIT GROUP

Michael Smurfit's 'equity is blood' speech, in which he implied that he would never sell shares in his business, was followed not many years later by him doing just that – as market forces conspired against him. The principle he expounded is worth taking into account for any business, though.

When your business is young, or indeed before you set it up, there is a temptation to give away large chunks of shares in the business, as at that point they are relatively worthless. Those self-same shares can in due course become very valuable, if you're any good. The original investor in the Body Shop chain with

Anita Roddick was a local businessman who turned his initial £10,000 stake into a multi-million-pound fortune.

Let's be clear: high degrees of risk should be rewarded, and I would be delighted if any small investor in O'Briens got that kind of return. I'm not suggesting that you hold on to all of your shares forever. After all, it is ultimately better to own just 30 percent of a really valuable company into which you have taken capital in order to help you expand than to own 100 percent of a company which is worth nothing but which you control absolutely.

If you really believe in your idea, though, you must believe that your shares will have a value some day. You will therefore be that much more wary, when your shares are in their 'little value' phase, about diluting your stake.

I should mention that Michael Smurfit was astute enough to invest in O'Briens at a time when others were reluctant to do so. He helped get us on to a sound footing – which, I hope, will be rewarded in times to come.

Give a man a fish, and you feed him for a day. Teach a man to fish, and you feed him for life

St Paul

How often do we end up doing a job ourselves because we know that we will do it just the way we want it done, and it's too much bother to show someone else how to do it? Yet I think the great leaders are those who teach us how to do things for ourselves. And growing any organisation has to involve the acceptance that we can't do everything on our own.

Jesus' very wise saying has direct relevance to the developed world helping the developing world, but it also has direct relevance for those of us charged with running an organisation. I am always finding myself doing jobs in our company, where the job is really someone else's. But because I don't take the time to think through the problem, it ends up costing me time, and probably annoying a colleague, who feels that I'm interfering. Instead, I could have trained a colleague to do the job by working through the issue with him or her. Training is an absolute pre-requisite for successful organisations.

Always try and employ people you think are better than you

ANONYMOUS

Companies that develop too much in the image and likeness of their founder are in danger of sinking. There is a natural tendency among some people to employ people who won't challenge them but will instead be subservient and sycophantic towards them. Because people also tend (if left unchecked) to recruit employees who are quite like them personally, you may end up in a business, as I did, where we were all happy and relaxed – but nobody was at home making sure we made some money.

I had a colleague just like that, who, after bitter experience, and despite the fact that I liked him personally, I had to let go. The colleague, who was in charge of a fairly large number of people in our organisation, seemed to be able to employ only people who were at best his equal, and more often inferior (at least in his eyes) to him.

The result was that we ended up in this department with a bunch of clones who wouldn't say boo to a goose, or speak up about anything, for fear that my colleague would demean their contribution. It wasn't a happy camp to be in.

In a different area, if you're a competitive sports player, you know instinctively that the way to improve your game is to play consistently against people who are better than you. It's not much fun losing, but you're learning all the time, and raising your own game.

The same applies to a work situation. Bringing into the organisation people who are intellectually stronger than you, or better marketers, or more effective with other people, can only increase the strength of your organisation. Really good people don't want to work with poor people, so a process of natural selection means that the poor people leave, thereby increasing the strength of the organisation.

12

Great Customer Service

How to give great service without paying for it

Let's start with two simple propositions. Firstly, people in employment are not parrots. Therefore, great customer service does not come from teaching people to be parrots. Rather, it comes from people being essentially happy in their work. Therefore, in order to give great customer service, you should look after the people who work with you.

Secondly, most people are not bad or dishonest. In almost any business you can think of, poor customer service is not given by bad people; poor customer service is given by badly managed people. The fault doesn't lie with the front-line staff but rather with the managers who are charged with looking after them. Great customer service comes from great owner/managers giving great leadership and creating a great environment for their workers. A visit to Kelly's Resort in Rosslare, run by Bill Kelly, or Adrian Baartels's Sheen Falls Lodge in Kenmare shows this great leadership in action.

I have a firm belief that only about half the reason our staff get out of bed in the morning is for the money they will make. Sure, we all need to eat and clothe ourselves and live somewhere, but once our basic needs are satisfied, we become concerned about other things: that's where the other half of the reason people go to work comes in. One important factor here is a person's sense of self-esteem, which is bolstered by the fact that they feel part of a team, share in the vision of where the business is supposed to be going, and share a common goal with their workmates. It is also important that they know they have a shoulder to lean on when things aren't going well, and will get a pat on the back when they do well – a sincere 'thank you' for a job well done.

I have seen many businesses over the years. In the poorly run ones, the owner or manager has said to me: 'You can't get good staff any more. The ones I have are useless. They will leave this job for fifty cent an hour more to go and work for the competition. Why should I bother training them, when they're just going to leave anyway?'

In the well-run ones, the owner/manager says something more like: 'I have a great team. They're really trying hard. I couldn't do it without them. They're hungry to learn, so I train them as efficiently as I can, accepting that, for most of them, they're not here for a career and will eventually leave.'

The same business, the staff paid the same rate. Guess which delivers better service?

Staff don't leave jobs for an extra fifty cent an hour. They leave because they're not treated with respect. Because the environment they are asked to work in is chaotic and they are not trained properly.

The people equation

I'm fortunate to be surrounded in my life by positive people. Whether it's a life partner, a close friend, or the workmates you spend your day with, if we have any choice about it, we'll go for our own type. Of course you need some balance in work. While it might be nice to surround myself with outgoing, gregarious people like myself who aren't that diligent about the detail of how something gets done, a business also needs methodical administrators in order to allow it to function correctly. That's why, in a work situation, you need to be careful about not letting some of the people around you employ people who are too like them.

Many business people I meet have a very one-track mind when it comes to employees. (Actually, I have always been uncomfortable about describing someone as 'my employee', or 'working for me'. It's a bit like describing Lulu as 'my wife'. I think it's old-fashioned language, which implies that you own the person – or your partner. I describe an employee of O'Briens as someone who works with me, not for me.)

These one-track-mind individuals argue that employees are there to get what they can for themselves and are only interested in the job for the money. It never surprises me to see businesses run by these people experiencing serious problems with their staff. It should come as no surprise either that these are the businesses with the worst customer service.

I believe that 95 percent of people are basically honest and that we should run the business for them, not for the 5 percent of people who might try to rip us off. It is an inescapable fact of building any sort of business that you have to trust people, in particular people who are working with you. You may be the best in the world in your particular field, but without a team you have only a limited amount of time in the day in which to achieve things. In fact, very few successful business people do it on their own. As we have seen, for people who work with you, less than half the reason they get out of bed in the morning is their wages. They do it because they are motivated, respected and trusted, and because they have responsibility, are cared for, and share a sense of vision about their work. I work with a fantastic bunch of people who I'm not ashamed to say I love.

The people I work with love being part of a winning team. (And they know they are, because we tell them all the time.) Our people are fired up about making a difference, achieving their potential, and being a part of a successful team. Other people are gobsmacked about how we have succeeded in this. Our staff are not paid in excess of market rates (although they do share in the financial success we enjoy), and we have very low staff turnover among the O'Briens support staff.

It's a fact of modern life that I spend more time with my work colleagues than I do with my partner, children or friends. As with my partner, children and friends, I would prefer to spend my time at work with people with whom I get on and share interests, and in a pleasant environment. A pleasant environment in a physical sense is not possible for everybody, but a pleasant environment in an emotional sense is possible for everyone.

While I give a lot of myself to my workmates to make sure they feel all these things, they pay me back tenfold in what they give back to me. This approach is also very good for the business, as we have a better chance of delivering the all-important customer service for which we strive.

So if you're serious about offering great customer service, why not start by looking at your attitude to the following:

Lead by example

The whole tone of the customer service in your business is set by you, the owner/manager and driver of the business. Paying for food and drink that you consume in your own store sends a strong message to your staff about how you respect your cash. How you personally deal with your customers – speaking about them respectfully (I heard one business associate describing his customers as being like the Taliban), holding a door open for them, thanking them for their business, cleaning up around them and listening to their comments, good or bad – sends powerful signals to your staff. If, on the other hand, you can't be bothered to get to know your customers, aren't respectful of them . . .

Praise in front of others, admonish in private

None of us likes getting a bollocking, and nobody likes it being done in front of other people. If it's necessary – and it often is – to straighten someone out about their performance or their attitude, you will earn far more respect from your employee if you do it in private. On the other hand, if you have something positive to say about someone, you should shout it from the

132

rafters. It is very important to catch your staff doing something right, as opposed to always having negative conversations with them.

I was walking through one of our stores one afternoon, when a customer I knew beckoned me over. Retailing, as I've said before, is one of those businesses where everybody is an expert in telling you how to run it, so I was fully expecting a lecture on one of our many shortcomings as a business.

Instead, this customer wanted to tell me about the brilliant service she had received from one of our staff members: Ann McLoughlin. The customer had come into the busy store struggling with a buggy and shopping. Ann had spotted her and asked some other customers if they would mind moving to an adjacent table, so that our happy customer could sit down without blocking the aisle. Ann had then taken her order and brought it down to her table. (O'Briens is mostly a self-service business.)

I was delighted with this feedback, and I decided to use the situation to my advantage. 'Ann McLoughlin, get over here this minute!' I roared in front of all the rest of the staff, and indeed a shop full of customers. Ann was mortified. She feared the worst as she made her way over to where I was standing. I put on my 'you're in big trouble' face as she approached. When she was standing beside me, I stood up and said: 'Ann McLoughlin, this lady beside me called me over to say that she's just had the best experience ever in O'Briens, because your customer service was exceptional. I know a lot of other people in this restaurant who work with you, or who are served by you, think you're fantastic too, so, as your boss, I just wanted to say "thank you".' Some people started to clap; our happy customer was beaming. Ann didn't know where to look: there were tears welling up in her eyes. It was a lovely moment for all the people in the store. Everybody felt a little better going back to work, or going home that evening, because they shared Ann's delight. (Sometime later, she told me that she had never been acknowledged like that before, by anyone, ever.) So shout your praise from the rooftops.

Communicate the vision

It's an old adage in business that's its very hard to get somewhere if you don't know where you're supposed to be going. To the extent that it's appropriate to communicate with your staff (obviously there's no point in sharing all your worries and concerns with them), it's generally worthwhile to let your colleagues in on the plan, and to get them to buy into it.

So we sit down with all our staff at the start of the year and talk about the year ahead. We get feedback from people working with us (which often leads to us coming up with a better plan), as well as understanding of the bigger picture, and how the different parts of the business – and, following that, the different people in the business – will interact.

Top teams know what they're about, have a sense of purpose, and are made aware of clearly measurable outcomes which they can get their heads around.

Regular 'thank you's

You can never say 'thank you' often enough. It should be obvious to any 'people person' that we respond very well to a pat on the back, and work harder and become more loyal as a result of frequent and sincere praise. Keeping a note of your associates (and that doesn't mean only your staff – watch how the customer service from your suppliers improves following regular and sincere praise, as appropriate), and remembering, every now and again, to single them out individually to thank them for a job well done will do more for the customer service in your organisation than almost anything else. In short, make your staff's time with you valuable.

Have a sense of fun

There's no rule that says business has to be boring. While there are certainly many boring aspects to some jobs, you, as the owner/operator, have the power to use humour to create a great atmosphere in your workplace. Fun tends to be infectious, so not only your staff but also your customers will end up with a smile on their faces.

Southwest Airlines, on the West Coast of the United States, built a reputation for their wacky staff, who wasted no opportunity to ham it up in front of their customers. The restaurant chain TGI Fridays allows staff to choose their own head coverings, which gives staff a sense of individuality while also providing a fun talking point with customers. Julian Richer, the founder of the Richer Sounds music-equipment chain, had a Rolls Royce available for staff who excelled in their work. These staff members were then able to bring the Rolls home and take their friends or parents for a spin. And any of us can create a great atmosphere at work by having a laugh with our customers.

Set the standard and continuously strive to reach it with your people

Any business will be defined firstly by your staff and secondly by your standards. It goes without saying that we should all be striving to improve our standards all the time. Having high standards is as much a personal approach to life as a business objective.

People often ask me how I maintain standards in O'Briens. It's a fair question. My answer is that, if you get the right people in as your franchise partners, the standards look after themselves. In other words, you can tie anyone up in knots with a legal agreement, but if the person has poor personal standards, whether in hygiene or business discipline, there is very little that can done to change that person. The right people will have high personal standards, which they will then encourage and coach their staff to achieve.

I suppose I am a perfectionist. I am never happy about the standards we achieve, and this can make things very difficult for the people who work with me. I think entrepreneurs are generally perfectionists, and the successful ones pass their perfectionism on to their staff. Being restless and unhappy about the standards that are reached means that you do not become complacent and are always trying to do things better.

Induct properly, train technically

During the height of Ireland's economic boom in the late 1990s, when there was essentially full employment, we had a kind of running joke in O'Briens about the difficulty of finding employees. A new recruit would be interviewed at 9 AM and asked to start work at 10. At noon, the new recruit was made a supervisor, and by 2 PM she had been appointed store manager. At 5 PM, the new recruit was gone, never to be seen again. While the joke is obviously exaggerated to make the point, it may be a bit close to the bone for some of us.

Imagine what a new recruit who is not given the time to figure out how the business works before he is asked to deal with customers thinks of his new employer. Imagine what your customer feels like being served by someone who, through no fault of their own, hasn't a clue how to look after them.

Taking time to induct somebody into the new business properly more than pays for itself in terms of the money you save by not having continually to advertise, interview and train a string of workers who start but don't last the pace.

In an ideal world (and, as we all know, it's not always ideal), a new recruit would start by having a tour of the business conducted by the boss or senior manager, where the way in which the business works is explained, and the new recruit is introduced to their colleagues and made feel welcome.

After that, a structured training programme would bring the new employee up to speed in an efficient and accountable way, so that they can start to contribute to the business as soon as possible. Doing the induction in this way demonstrates the professionalism of your organisation while hugely increasing your chances of retaining that person, especially if they're good.

Even in what appears to be a simple business, like O'Briens, where we have a relatively high staff turnover at the retail level, you can easily see, from spending five minutes in the store, the standards that are set in terms of training the staff.

Know your workmates personally

Given the number of people with whom you will be trying to keep a close relationship, it pays to be interested in their life outside the business environment.

For many years in the early days of O'Briens, I had a young girl working with me called Mary Devine (not her real name). Mary, who was sixteen and had dropped out of the education system, was very bright and hard-working. Over the years, I have become very fond of some staff that I have worked with; Mary was one of those people. I delighted in the fact that she broke all the stereotypes associated with a girl from her background. She came from a part of Dublin which at the time had 40 percent unemployment. It wasn't the green fields and private schools of south County Dublin where she was reared. Her father was unemployed, and the family was poor. Despite that, she was driven to get on, and did so, while becoming very loyal to me personally. She was one of the few people in the business I trusted absolutely.

Mary rapidly became a supervisor and then, at the age of just seventeen, a store manager in one of our busy downtown stores, where she managed a mixed crew of staff, mostly very well. Unfortunately, Mary had a lowlife boyfriend, and I was saddened to see her promising career falter when, still aged only seventeen, she came to tell me she was pregnant. She worked on for as long as she could, and shortly thereafter gave birth to a baby boy, James (again, not his real name). Despite the fact that she was happy to be a mother, her relationship with her boyfriend wasn't going well, and he was violent towards her. She was also living at home and didn't get on too well with her father. James turned out to be hyperactive, and she found it very difficult to cope with things.

When James was about six months old, she moved out of her parents' home and moved in with her boyfriend. As soon as she could arrange for her mother to help out with minding the baby, she came back to O'Briens to work part-time. Mary, I knew, found sanity and order in work where there was none in her private life; in that sense work was her escape from her own reality and the mess she was in.

One morning, I received a call from one of our staff to say that there was no one to let them in to work. Because some of the stores had been open consistently late recently, and we had had a staff meeting about the issue, I was livid. It happened to be Mary's store, and unfortunately, I was beyond reason. I went down to open the store myself, and when Mary turned up at 10 AM, two and a half hours late, without having phoned to explain herself, I let her have it. I was in no mood for excuses.

She burst into tears. It turned out that her boyfriend had beaten her up the night before. She had had to leave her flat, with the baby, after midnight and try to get into a women's refuge. The first one she tried was full, and they sent her in her nightclothes, in a taxi, to a second one, where they took her in. She had been so upset that they had given her a sedative to calm her down, and she had overslept. When she had awoken, she had to go back to her flat to get some clothes and the baby's things.

As soon as I heard this, I felt awful. Here I was reading her the riot act, when she had just been through the most dreadful experience. It taught me that you never really know what's going on in someone's private life. I have taken it onboard as one of life's lessons.

If you only take three things from this chapter . . .

1 When it comes to giving great customer service, lead by example

2 Praise in front of others, admonish in private

3 Induct properly, train technically

Most important of all . . .

You can never say 'thank you' often enough

13

Get a Life

Keeping perspective in your business and personal lives

No one ever on their deathbed said: 'I wish I'd spent more time at the office'

ANONYMOUS

I'm not sure why a chapter dealing with keeping a balanced life should make it into a business book, but our lives and work are so intertwined these days that, for most people, separating them is difficult. I think the majority of us would like to look back on our lives as having been defined by something other than the sentence: 'He was a very hard worker.' Keeping perspective will lead to you having a fuller, more rounded life and, I suspect, will contribute to you having a more successful business venture as well.

I remember, I suspect with rose-tinted glasses, the working life my father Frank appeared to have. My father was a lawyer, with an office in a lovely old Georgian building on the banks of the Liffey in Dublin's city centre. I remember visiting his office as a small boy. His working day seemed to consist at that time of arriving at the office around 10 AM. A fire would have been lit in his room, and a cup of tea, served from what were quaintly known as the Cherryhound cups, would immediately be served.

(Cherryhound Estates was a company of which Frank was a director at the time; the cups were kept for the board meetings.) He would do some work until about 12.30, when he would meet up with some of his pals or legal acquaintances for a long, liquid lunch at one of the city's gentlemen's clubs. After arriving back at work at about 3.30, slightly the worse for wear, he would put in a strenuous hour and a half or so's work before heading home for the evening. On his arrival home, he would be greeted like a long-lost hero by my mother and put sitting down in front of the fire with a gin and tonic while his dinner was prepared.

My Dad was proud of the fact that his firm, Croskerrys, was reputed to be the oldest law firm in Dublin. He told a funny story about his boss, who never got to grips with that new-fangled invention, the telephone. In fact, old man Croskerry never used the phone, and refused to have one in his room. When clients rang to speak to him, he used to have his secretary relay messages to him; he would then give his secretary the necessary instructions, which she would relay to the client.

I don't think my father was unusual in his lifestyle: that's the way professional people lived and worked then. Although it seems idyllic, I'm sure that it brought its own problems, and that my father's life was subject to very similar stresses and strains to the ones we experience today. What he did appear to have, however, was some balance between work and play – which a lot of us seem to have lost.

As a general rule, I encourage my workmates to have a full life outside work. An unbalanced approach to work will of course affect a person's personal life, whereas an individual's personal development through work is the thing that is important for them. It's a truism that no one ever complained on their deathbed: 'I wish I'd spent more time at the office.' Instead, people regret all the other things they should have done – spent more time with their children, developed hobbies, had more time for other people, their partners or friends – whatever.

Successful, modern businesses recognise that being good to staff is good business. Making people's personal development through work the goal, rather than the work being the end in itself, produces better results: better spirit in the organisation, a greater sense of community in a shared vision and, God forbid, the organisation making more money as a result. We at O'Briens recognise that we spend far more time together as a work team than we do as individuals with our partners, friends or family. That work provides our sense of community. That, if we're going to spend most of our time at work, we should do it in a pleasant environment, where we have fun, and there are opportunities to socialise (after all, some of our closest friendships are with our workmates).

We have to work hard as employers to try to ensure that our people develop balance in their lives, and so our interaction becomes a way of life. We don't just make sandwiches and coffee; we work, play and eat together, as well as having separate and private personal lives.

Having said that, I have little time for people who go completely the opposite way and take the attitude that 'I want to give up work to spend more time with the children.' Does no one ever think of the poor children in this situation? In my limited experience, my kids want to spend a relatively short time in the morning with me and a longer period in the evening, and have a day out with their parents at the weekend, as well as holidays. If I tried to spend any more time than that with them, they'd think there was something wrong with me. They need to develop their own relationships and find their feet as people, without the constant and intrusive presence of mummy and daddy.

I don't think we need to put ourselves under as much pressure, in terms of how we spend our time, as we seem to think society expects us to. We think that, if we're not burning the midnight oil, we're not maximising our potential. What rubbish! Admittedly, I would consider myself to be a lazy person, but a productive eight-hour day is far better than a holier-than-thou, and possibly fairly unproductive, twelve-hour one. Sure, if the chips are down, we expect our people to put in the hours, but not all the time.

Lulu and I have made our weekends sacrosanct. We don't work at weekends, except for a small number of clearly defined work weekends through the year. I try to travel between Tuesday and Thursday, and I am out and about most weeks, but if I'm around on Monday and Friday, and at the weekend, I feel I'm not missing out on too much. We have a family Sunday roast most weeks. I have started taking the whole of August off for a family month at our home in Sligo in the west of Ireland. I don't feel the need to ring up the O'Briens head office on a daily or weekly basis to check on what's happening. This has the added benefit of encouraging the people who work with you to make their own decisions and stand over them. Last year, I left the office for my month in Sligo, with the instruction that, if I was to be disturbed, it had better be for a good reason. People took the message onboard, and I wasn't disturbed once. It was pure bliss: I had time to work on my fishing and gardening – important stuff. Lulu sometimes brings work home to read. I strongly disapprove of this, and almost never do it, particularly at weekends. And you know, I don't think we miss too much. I certainly feel I spend as much good time with my partner and kids as my parents did with me. It takes a lot of organising to make it work – which, in truth, Lulu does most of – but it works for us.

So, herewith Brody's guide to getting a life:

Get organised

As with any aspect of your business, you have to plan the various aspects of your life. Getting organised, thinking ahead and planning your leisure time will mean that you have a much better chance of taking time off. Applying the principles set out in Chapter 6 will be a solid start.

Do something for someone else

Doesn't it make you feel good inside when you do something nice for someone else? The very act of not thinking about yourself or your business first will produce lots of positive energy for you in return. If that something you do is for someone associated with the business like a customer or co-worker, then even better.

Learn how to switch off

I'm convinced that time spent away from work gives you a helpful perspective on your working life and your business. Not everybody has the ability to make a clear distinction between work and play, but that doesn't mean you shouldn't try to do so.

Actually switch off your computer, mobile phone, Blackberry personal organiser and handheld computer. I know far too many business people who can't switch off their mobile communications when on holidays. What's wrong with them? I suppose it's possible for a very few of us that we might need to keep in constant touch with the office while we're on holiday (I wouldn't include myself in this group) or that, from time to time, something important might require our input. But most people in this situation have become information junkies and simply can't let go.

Your holiday time is supposed to be a period for recharging your batteries, paying attention to your family and thinking about other things – like where you're going with your life. Instead, we allow ourselves to be dominated by little machines and don't give ourselves the mental space we need.

Get a life! Be radical and just turn the gadgets off – all of them. Treat yourself like an alcoholic: take it one day at a time and just resist the temptation. Whenever you feel the urge coming on you, go and visit a historic monument, make love to your partner, play with the kids, read a book – do what you're supposed to be doing!

Get a hobby: be good at something

Why is there an expectation that, if you want to be serious about business, you shouldn't have outside interests? That the only way to succeed in business is by working harder than anyone else and being completely focused on what you are doing. Developing a hobby makes you a much more interesting person, especially to those who share your hobby.

Dealing with stress

It's only to be expected that, from time to time, we will get ourselves into stressful situations. Running a business means that you have to deal with more of these situations, and at more frequent intervals. Positive stress can be enjoyable, as you get the good breaks and enjoy them, but negative stress can put us under great mental and physical strain.

Then there are the immediate stressors, like the bank manager threatening to bounce a cheque or a physical confrontation with a customer, and slow-burning stressors, like the business being in trouble and the thought that, if you don't do something, you mightn't be in business in a year's time.

Physical manifestations of stress, like sweaty hands and a racing heart, are reinforced by the mental aspects of stress: a mind that won't stay still, an inability to keep perspective on a problem, and the mind shutting out everything except the immediate problem. This isn't good for the business: you can make really bad decisions when you're under stress, and it's certainly not good for the mind and body.

A lot of my stress is created by fear of the unknown. As I lie awake in bed at night, I sometimes rehearse the different possible outcomes of a particular situation; this causes my mind to race along, I suppose because it is seeking solutions to perceived problems.

I haven't become expert at dealing with stress, but some things seem to work better than others. Like distracting yourself by doing something completely different. Or talking the problem over with someone whose opinion you respect. Or indeed writing down the pros and cons of the situation: this exercise in itself can help resolve things in your mind.

I have also found it useful, when I am being put under

pressure to make a decision but am uncertain about what decision to make, to do nothing. Often the obvious decision becomes clearer the following day, or something else happens and the problem sorts itself out.

Keep your friends

I went through a period of work which was so intense that, when I took a little time off to spend with my friends, I couldn't think of anything to talk about except coleslaw and sandwich marketing. This is not helpful if you want to keep your friends close to you. I have to force myself to stop talking about me, me, me and to listen to what's going on in other people's lives. I put it in my annual plan to spend some time with the people I feel closest to: if I didn't plan it, it wouldn't happen.

Eat well

I have reached an age when I realise that, if I live the rest of my life the way I have lived it so far, I may not be for this world too much longer. I am very conscious of the fact that my Dad died at fifty-six: young in today's terms. In the last couple of years, I have started to take care of my body a little better. There are many different diets, apart from the ones for people with weight problems, that can help you eat better. Choose one that suits you. I have found some simple things that have helped me and have given me more vitality. And if they're simple, I'm less likely to forget them and will have more chance of applying them successfully.

For example, I only eat fruit until midday because it is easier than other foods for the body to digest, and my body isn't struggling to digest a big meal when I should be at my most productive. (By the way, have you tried one of our delicious O'Briens smoothies!) I don't drink fluids with my meals and I leave a gap of at least ten minutes between eating and drinking. I have given up drinking milk and eating breakfast cereals. This is working for me at the moment, anyway. I'm not a complete anorak, however, and I do splash out on a big Irish breakfast occasionally. I have also adapted the fluid-with-meals rule to exclude wine – as I say, it works for me.

Just thinking about it is the first step. Your body needs your love, and if you love it, it will perform better. It won't let you down and should last for ages.

Go for a walk

In fact, any form of exercise will do. It's a sad reality that, in most of our urban-based work, the harder we work, the less we work out, and the more unfit we become. Of course, when starting or running a small business, we make every possible excuse as to why we don't have time to exercise. I tried joining a gym a few years ago. It wasn't for me. I was bored to tears cycling on a treadmill or lifting weights. I decided that what bored me was doing the exercise on my own.

A few years ago, I started a sponsored cycle across Ireland for charity. It's held each year in June or July. This means that, in about February or March, I have to start training for it. (I made the mistake the first year of not training for it properly and I thought near the end that I was about to die.) Having to focus on getting ready means that I have to discipline myself to get out at least a couple of times a week at the start of the programme, then build up to more strenuous efforts nearer the time. It feels good and gets me reasonably fit for at least part of the year. The event itself is great fun, and I know a lot of the people who do it get as much out of it as I do. That's part of the reason they come back every year – because it provides a focus for part of their lives and helps them improve their physical fitness.

It's horses for courses. As you get older, there are no excuses. We have to do whatever it takes to look after our bodies and our minds so that we get the most out of them.

Make the time to go and do something physical. Build it into your routine. Keep it simple. Find something you enjoy doing and make the decision to become good at it.

146

Look around you

It's a beautiful world! Everybody is doing different things. They have their own lives and problems. Somebody is always worse off than you. The world doesn't revolve around you and your life. I know how extraordinary I find it that, after a period of intense work, there is another world out there. When we're really busy, we tend to forget about the outside world and neglect things that, in the normal course of events, would be important to us.

Be the leader — and lead

Have you noticed the way people react to good leadership in a positive way? The jobs that I consider the most important are giving our co-workers an idea of what the future can be like and a sense of community in the sharing out of tasks, and helping them to achieve. There are wonderful examples of leadership, of people with little more than a burning vision and the ability to inspire others to join them, who have succeeded against what appeared to be insurmountable odds.

They inspire me (and others) to think outside the narrow scope of our own experiences and to imagine what is possible. And to reach further and higher than logic dictates we are able to do.

Honesty and integrity seem for many to be forgotten traits. 'My word is my bond': those words used to mean something. But they haven't really been forgotten by most of the people I deal with. It's not a dead subject. In truth, it's the most important aspect of deal-making: the ability to consummate a relationship is far more important than what a highfalutin legal document might say.

I love to meet passionate people, even when I don't agree with them. Their passion for their subject, whether it's business, art, charity, sport, or whatever, shows in the enthusiasm, animation and energy they display.

I was at a management-training course a few years ago where

the trainer talked about this passion and enthusiasm. He described a man working in the accounts office of a supermarket who turned in for work each day, did his work (which he wasn't greatly excited about) and went home. When he got home, he immediately changed into his football jersey, hat and scarf, and went off to support his local team in the soccer league. On the way to the match, he met his pals and talked enthusiastically about the forthcoming game. At the ground, he was on his feet for most of the game, shouting, roaring or singing, depending on what was going on on the pitch. He laughed and cried, was elated and depressed, all in the space of ninety minutes.

What made him so passionate and enthusiastic about the soccer, while he merely existed at work? Could it be that soccer provided him with his sense of belonging and community, through the strip all the supporters wore and due to the fact that he sat in a particular part of the stadium? That there were easily measurable goals in terms of the team's position in the league, and specifically the score in the match. He was able to respond to the leadership of the manager and players on the field, and share in their success when they had secured victory. He also had his status within his own peer group confirmed, as he shared with them the team's trials and tribulations. Notice that money isn't a factor here. Could it be that all of these things were provided by football, and none of them by his working life?

I have always thought that this story is a great way of describing the difference between an organisation where there is passion and one where there isn't. And it's leaders who inspire passion.

If you only take three things from this chapter . . .

1   Don't bring work home

2   Eat well and take plenty of exercise

3   Don't forget to spend time doing the things you enjoy

Most important of all . . .

Learn how to switch off – and then actually switch off your machines

14

Ownership and Responsibility

Who's really in charge
of running your business?

Starting up the O'Briens business was by far the hardest thing I have ever done in my now fairly long life. I thought I knew it all. I had spent eight years running the Prontaprint business in Ireland, knew about the importance of site selection, had gained some experience in retail marketing and had developed a sound business concept. I knew the importance of a good business plan, and having enough money for the project (although in the business textbooks, I had never come across my particular method of fund-raising!).

I had that youthful male arrogance which said that I knew everything, that nobody else could teach me anything, and that I was so good at what I did that I simply couldn't fail. In short, external factors aside, there was no reason for the business not to succeed.

But it didn't succeed. The early years of the business were disastrous: not just bad but chronically awful. And, worse than that, there was nobody else to blame: I had started, stirred and created the mess I was in myself. Sure, I could have blamed the banks, or the fact that the market wasn't ready for our products, or that my competitors tried to put me out of business, but in truth my problems were of my own making. The first positive step I took in terms of sorting things out was to admit to myself that I hadn't been very good at it thus far.

Few people mention the 'driver' factor when starting a new business. The driver of the business is the person who dreams up the idea, executes it, and steers the business during its formative years. Commentators talk about the success of a new business venture being dependent on the state of the economy, or the market for widgets, or the need to secure the necessary finance, or the technical qualities of a particular product compared with what is already in the market.

You hardly ever hear people talking about the ability of the company's founder to run the damned thing. External factors always have some influence on the success of a venture, but the single most important factor in my experience is the quality of the driver, or owner, of the business.

Our second O'Briens store in the UK was opened in Cambridge by a young couple called Rob and Carol Shields. It was the couple's first ever attempt to run their own business. Prior to joining O'Briens, Rob, a Geordie, had worked as a clerk of works involved in motorway construction. I think they were very brave. Here they were, moving to a strange town to set up a new business for the first time, with a fledgling Irish sandwich-bar chain which had yet to prove itself in Britain. I visited Cambridge with them and walked the streets of the city to try to find a suitable location for the store. After some months of searching, we found a good location not far from the city centre, just outside the gates of one of the university colleges.

We opened the store in 1996, and Rob and Carol worked extremely hard to try to make the business a success. But six months after opening, it wasn't really happening. Sales were less than anticipated, and the money the couple had borrowed from the bank was running out. Rob and Carol were concerned; I was *very* concerned, as there was a real possibility that the problem was our new Irish brand. Often, when a new store isn't working, it can be apparent that the new operators are having personal difficulties running the store. But in this case, I was convinced that Rob and Carol were doing an excellent job. This was why I was so worried.

A meeting was arranged in Cambridge with Rob and Carol's financial advisers, and we debated what to do about the situation. I was stumped. These were good people, trying to operate the business according to the approach laid down in our operations manuals, and it wasn't working. Because theirs was one of the first stores in Britain, I began to have doubts about the viability of the O'Briens concept in the UK. Maybe people didn't like the Irish brand, or the sandwiches. The meeting was inconclusive, and I returned to Ireland seriously concerned about the whole future of the company in the UK.

Meanwhile, Rob realised that he was in trouble and that, if he didn't do something about it, he was going to go bust. To his credit, he never blamed O'Briens for his predicament, but as far as I was concerned, we were very responsible for the situation he and Carol found themselves in. We had persuaded them to trust us with their life savings, and we were letting them down.

Rob decided that the business was not going to survive on the store sales alone, so he put on his best bib and tucker and started knocking on doors in the area around his store, offering a delivery service for meetings, receptions, training courses and the like. His positive attitude to getting out there and doing whatever it took to succeed made the crucial difference. Slowly, he began to turn the business around. Soon afterwards, the store started to break even overall, and they were on their way. Today, Rob and Carol are enjoying the fruits of their success after building up and selling four O'Brien's units in Cambridge.

Rob and Carol should, by rights, have failed. They had every excuse to do so. But Rob took ownership of the problem and succeeded where many people would have given up. I have no doubt that a lesser person than Rob would not have survived to tell the tale. It proved to me forever more the importance of the 'business driver'.

Owner/managers are responsible for everything to do with their businesses, but to help you focus on what's most important, you could try prioritising the following points:

Cash is king

Cash has rightly been described as the oil that makes the wheels of commerce turn. You can be so busy running around doing other things that keeping an eye on the cash slips way down the priority list, until it's too late to do anything about it. A surprising number of businesses run out of cash before they become established. There are many and varied reasons for this, from having little or no credit control, so that some customers take advantage of you, to not making sure you're achieving the margins you need in order to generate enough cash. Lack of cash control signifies lack of control of the business; this means that there's no one in charge.

What gets measured gets done

You need to set clearly defined targets for yourself and those working with you and constantly measure yourself against these targets to see how you're doing. Setting targets is part of the planning process. All businesses – not just new business start-ups – should have a plan for each year. Even a small business should have a simple one-page plan setting out clearly defined objectives for the year ahead. This should then be shared with those working with you. If you show someone how to do a job, or what the overall plan is, and they agree with your expectations of them, there are no excuses.

This is the reason most medium-sized businesses do monthly management accounts. Targets are set, broken down into monthly objectives, and then the accounts measure the actual performance of the business.

You have to communicate your vision

If you expect the people who work with you to buy into your grand plan for the business, you need to tell them what that plan is. When we want to achieve something in O'Briens, the first thing we do is set clear long-term – or 'big picture' – goals, and then break these goals down into more manageable, bite-sized chunks. In management, there is the old story about 'eating an elephant'. If you imagine trying to eat an elephant in one go, it's a daunting task, impossible to achieve. If you break the elephant down into bite-sized chunks, however, you can eventually achieve your goal and eat the elephant.

In O'Briens, our 'elephant' is to open one thousand stores over a set period of time. We have broken that big-picture goal down into smaller goals (the bite-sized chunks), which relate to how many stores we can open in one year. Everyone in the company has a fairly clear sense of both our big-picture goal and our short-term objectives en route to achieving that goal.

One of the exercises we go through, usually annually, is a process of visualisation that involves imagining what the company will look like in one or two years' time, as opposed to what it looks like now. The visualisation exercise enables us to imagine what the various departments in the business would look like if the company was twice the size it is now. For example, what will having double the number of stores mean for our sales and marketing department? How will the operations department be affected? How will our financial people administer a bigger business? Will the management structure that is currently in place be sufficient as the company grows? How will the support we offer our franchise partners change?

By examining, through this visualisation exercise, all the issues that will affect our organisation and the likely impact that its expanded size will have on it, we can come up with a 'big plan'. In that way, when the changes happen, they will not come as a surprise to the company's staff. Secondly, we're getting our staff to buy into the vision, and the part they can play in O'Briens making the transition to a business twice the size it is at the moment.

One of the things I think is particularly noticeable when you come into contact with O'Briens staff is the fact that no one is frightened by the prospect of running a chain of one thousand stores. When you think of this in an Irish context, that is a huge business – one that's outside the experience of almost all Irish business people. By sharing our vision with everyone in the company and using these visualisation exercises, our people are prepared, confident, and aware of the part they have to play in growing the business.

Inspire by example

Your workmates will soon work out whether you are willing to lead by example, and that will affect what they are prepared to do for you. For example, when I visit one of our stores, if I see a dirty floor or table, I generally just clean it up myself. This sends a message to the store owner that I am prepared to put in the work on the ground myself – quite literally! For the same reason, I would always allow a paying customer to be served before me in an O'Briens store: this sends out a signal about treating people correctly. It tends to be the little things you do rather than the big gestures that have the best effect.

Delegate, and trust people – but check, just in case

It's impossible to get on in business without trusting people. Except in the smallest of businesses, your job is to manage; it's other people's job to do. The more time you do the 'doing', the less time you will have to manage.

So, delegate, but don't assume that, just because you have delegated, the job is done. A good example of this is with the use of e-mails. Have you noticed certain people's tendency to send an e-mail and then assume the job is done? I don't know how things are for you, but I typically get about forty e-mails a day, and I know that I don't read all of them in the detail I should. And if I don't, how can I expect my colleagues to do so? So, after sending an e-mail, I usually phone a little later to see whether a particular job has been done.

155

You've got to do whatever it takes

As you have read elsewhere in this book, the only certainty when it comes to starting a new business is the uncertainty involved. These businesses almost never go according to plan. Having come up with the idea and got the project off the ground, you can't afford not to see the business through to fruition. Rob and Carol's story above is an example of the importance of doing whatever it takes to make the business a success.

No one is likely to ride to your rescue, especially if the problems are the result of your own mistakes or negligence. So put the excuses and the negativity aside and decide that you're just going to go for it. Inform those around you and inspire them to row in behind you, and believe in yourself.

It's not a democracy

Everyone's leadership style is different. I think my personal style is to seek a consensus approach – although those who work with me may think differently! 'Tough but fair' seems to be what a good leader should aim for. 'Tough' because a business is not a democracy, and sometimes tough, unpopular decisions have to be taken; and 'fair' in the sense that you should try to take the effect that a particular decision will have on people into account.

As the 'leader' of O'Briens, I have a fairly clear idea about where we should be going. Not everyone around me agrees with that vision, or the way in which we are executing it, and that's fair enough. But as long as I'm running the show, I think it's my duty not to get distracted by people who don't agree with it. Sure, a leader should be mature enough to change track if it is clearly demonstrated that they are wrong, but otherwise it's their vision of how things should be that has helped get the business to where it is.

Two examples of me digging my heels in were over selling panini and selling chips. I won't allow either of them on the menu in O'Briens stores because, in the case of panini, all the other sandwich bars sell them and we need to be different, and in the case of chips, they're deep-fried and therefore unhealthy, and we promote O'Briens meals as a healthy type of fast food.

Now, even though I didn't agree to putting panini on the menu, there was clearly a demand for a hot sandwich, so we invented a product that was uniquely ours, called a Toostie™, which satisfied all the requirements of a panini without having to be more of the same.

If you feel you're right, there's a good chance you are and you owe it to yourself to see it through, and to hell with the naysayers!

If you only take three things from this chapter . . .

1   Communicate your vision

2   Inspire by example

3   Delegate, and trust people – but also check that something's been done

Most important of all . . .

You have to do whatever it takes

15

Don't Believe Your Own PR

How to know how your business is really doing

I've often been asked when O'Briens turned the corner and I knew things were going to be OK and the company had a viable future. From the PR we had been putting out, we had created the impression that we were a very successful business. Bear in mind that I lost money for the first six years – longer than most business start-ups do. For me, the change came when Tom Cunningham, our first-ever franchise partner, asked me whether he could open a second O'Briens store.

Tom is an accountant from Mayo, and it had taken a fair bit of persuasion on our part to get him to become our first franchise partner. At the time, I had a small number of stores already set up which I was running myself. I had written my franchise manual but was finding it hard to interest anybody in becoming a guinea pig for the idea and opening the first store. I decided that, in order to get the business off the ground, probably the smartest thing for me to do was to sell one of the existing stores – one which had a proven track record of sales and profitability.

The store I decided on was my best one, in the St Stephen's Green Shopping Centre. This store had a newsagent's attached to it. (I had no interest in running the newsagent's, but at the time it was probably the most valuable part of the business.) I advertised to sell, and Tom, who was interested in buying the newsagent's, came to talk to me. I explained that I was trying to start a franchise business built around a sandwich bar but that the newsagent's didn't really fit into my plan. I asked Tom if he'd be interested in becoming the first O'Briens franchise partner. To sweeten the deal, I said I wouldn't charge him any royalties (a percentage of sales the franchisee pays us for using the O'Briens name) unless I could sell three more franchises, and I wouldn't charge him any royalties at all on the newsagent's.

From Tom's point of view, this wasn't an unattractive proposition. He got to buy the newsagent business outright with no strings attached and had somebody working with him to develop the food side of the business, where the profit was. As well as that, if the O'Briens business couldn't be developed, he wouldn't have to pay anything by way of royalty, as we had agreed.

Tom eventually agreed, and that crucial first sale got the business off the ground and gave other people the confidence to make similar investments. It wasn't long before three franchises had been sold, and Tom, true to his word, started paying his royalties. When he came to me sometime later and said that he wanted to open a second store, I knew that the business had great possibilities. It can be relatively easy to sell a store to somebody who doesn't know much about a business, but an intelligent man like Tom wouldn't go ahead and buy a second business if he wasn't reasonably happy with the way the first one was going.

Tom went on to open another three O'Brien's stores before eventually scaling the business back to one, which he runs successfully to this day, more than ten years after we got into bed together, as it were.

The Manchester United manager Alex Ferguson said: 'Great teams don't just win trophies; great teams *retain* their trophies.' It's possible to win a trophy once or make a sale through a fluke or through good salesmanship. Being able to do so more than once takes the strength and depth that only a great team has.

Don't believe your own PR

We at O'Briens have always worked hard to create in the minds of our staff and the public a positive vibe abut the business. This has involved us creating and distributing very positive PR. This PR hasn't always been strictly true. There were periods when the business wasn't doing particularly well and we were still pumping out the positive stories. Some people running businesses get caught up in the hype they themselves have created. It's very tempting, with the heightened publicity you are receiving, and the consequent effect on your ego, to lose the run of yourself.

Always be optimistic, even when things aren't going well

There are inevitably times in the life of any business when things do not go according to plan. For instance, just before I was to make a sales presentation to a prospective franchise partner, I got a call from my bank manager to tell me they were calling in my overdraft. . . . Well, if you are to succeed with your sales presentation, you have to put your best foot forward, put on a cheery face and radiate optimism for your meeting – while you may actually be churning up inside as you try to figure a way out of your predicament.

At various times, I couldn't share with our team all the trouble we were in. A leader's job is to inspire confidence; if I'd let the rest of the team know the real story about the business, they would probably have started looking for new jobs. You always have to be optimistic, even when everyone around you is telling you you're mad.

Aim for long-term success

Lots of businesses seem like they are a licence to print money. The dot-com boom was a typical example. It appeared that you only had to add '.com' to your name, dream up some wheeze that said you had 'first mover advantage', and you were off. I have seen very few businesses that have enjoyed overnight success, however, and some of the great success stories of our time come from companies that had a miserably difficult and protracted start-up period.

In our business, we understood that what we wanted to build would take time and that this would come only from making our franchisees successful. Knowing that, I wasn't in a hurry (although it would have been nice if it hadn't taken quite as long as it did!). Slowly and carefully, we tried to bring the right people into the business and do whatever it took to help them achieve profitability. We needed them to know that we would do just about anything for them, and that they would be treated respectfully and seriously.

It takes time to get your business right. To make mistakes and recover from them. To discover what you're good at and what you're not so good at, and to bring in people who can complement your strengths.

Understand the key drivers for your business

There are particular aspects of the running of your business that are critical to its success. For Jay Bourke and Eoin Foyle, who rescued Bewley's on Grafton Street in Dublin, it was understanding what their peer group wanted from a midmarket bar-and-restaurant business. For Ronan McNamee and Pat Loughrey, the guys who started the Cuisine de France business, it was providing a really good-quality part-baked product which could be finished off in the local corner store.

Understanding the key drivers for your business will show you what you should concentrate your management time on – even if that means ignoring what's biting you on the bum at that particular moment.

Actively listen to customers, staff and suppliers

Getting caught up in the day-to-day hassles of running an organisation can divorce you from what's actually happening on the ground. You need to take time out to listen to what your stake-holders are saying. In the middle of the clutter, there may be a message for you, which it's important you know about.

Forget about what the competition is doing

It's easy to spend your time watching what the competition are up to, particularly if your business is not doing very well. I can remember standing outside a competitor's café in Mary Street wondering what he was doing to fill his place up that I wasn't. I got very upset about it for a while and wasn't able to do anything positive about my own situation. I was paralyzed by the success of the competition; when I reacted to what they were doing, it was in a knee-jerk fashion. Their prices were lower, so I reduced mine. It made no difference. They were doing cooked breakfasts, so I tried cooked breakfasts. Our sales actually went down. We stopped doing cooked breakfasts. Meanwhile, I lost sight of the big picture. We were supposed to be the best upmarket sand-wich-and-coffee house in Dublin. Cooked breakfasts were no part of the game plan.

If you concentrate on your own game and don't lose sight of your reason for being, you'll get it right eventually.

Employ the best professional advice
you can afford

Usually, when we're starting up in business, we don't have many contacts in the legal and financial world, and we end up with family members or friends of friends as advisers. You may be lucky and end up with someone really great this way, but you might not. The lawyer who handled the sale of your house may not be the best person to handle your business affairs.

Your professional advisers, apart from providing a legally required service like preparing accounts or agreeing a lease on a business premises, also act as informal mentors to the business. Your accountant, for example, may also act for businesses in a similar field to yours and be able to let you have the benefit of that experience (without, of course, breaking client confidentiality). An accountant can be an invaluable source of advice as you plan and execute your business strategy. Like any mentors, they also have the great advantage of being dispassionate and not involved with your business on a day-to-day basis.

Professional advisers come with a health warning, though. They're not all as expert as they think they are, and they can give bad advice as well as good. Tread carefully, and remember that it's your decisions, rather than somebody else's, that have got you this far.

Get into the habit of doing monthly management accounts

I and many people like me find doing accounts boring and tend to leave them till the last possible moment. They inevitably slip down the priority list and as a consequence end up taking more time and causing more hassle than if they had been dealt with in the same way that other aspects of the business are dealt with.

I have seen people in business – indeed, I did it myself at the beginning – arriving into their accountants' to do their accounts with large black plastic sacks full of invoices, credit notes, delivery notes, chequebook stubs, bank statements and unopened envelopes containing who-knows-what. This is not good.

Even the smallest business needs to know how it's doing. If doing your own books is not your cup of tea (not having time to do them is not an excuse – with proper organization, anything is possible), or you're just not prepared to do them, then you should arrange to get a bookkeeper to set everything up before you start. Bookkeepers are a grade down from accountants and so usually charge less than a full-blown accounting firm would. You may need an accountant to sign off on your annual accounts, but your bookkeeper can prepare everything for him.

Being disciplined about preparing monthly accounts forces you to get your paperwork into a decent shape every few weeks, means that you are less likely to be stuck with penalties for late

PAYE and VAT returns and, most importantly, enables you to measure the financial performance of the enterprise so that you really know what's going on and can take remedial action as appropriate.

Understand and monitor the different areas of your business

As we have discussed already, we all have a natural tendency to concentrate on the things that interest us. Keeping a check on the main area of your business every month or so, perhaps at the same time as you review your monthly management accounts, is a great idea. A new term for this is 'KPIs', or 'Key Performance Indicators'. In a bank, the KPIs to watch could be the growth in the number of loans on the books and the rate of default of high-risk loans. In a retail business, it might be the number and volume of transactions, gross margins and staff costs. Other areas to consider are:

Finance

Monthly management accounts, cash flow, creditor days, PAYE and VAT payments or refunds due, relationships with accounting staff (creditor days are the number of days on average it takes your customers to pay you; forty-five days or less is good in a business which gives credit)

Human resources

Increase or decrease staff levels, holiday planning, disciplinary issues, staff meetings, incentive programmes, salary reviews, appraisals

Marketing and sales promotions

Planning promotions, looking after existing customers, measuring the effectiveness of campaigns, PR activity, relationships with sales staff

Production

Review of processes, relationships with production staff, wastage reports, stocktaking, production-area cleanliness, health and safety, purchasing

Research and development

New-product development programme, pricing to achieve margin, existing product development, competition monitoring, visiting trade shows, reading trade press

Keep control of costs

Nothing ever seems to cost what it was envisaged it would at start-up. Capital costs have a habit of spiralling upwards, and operating costs take an age to settle down to a predictable level. This all comes back to making sure you control your business and not the other way around. If you don't know how you're doing, it's very hard to do anything about it. I make no apology for harping on about the need for an owner/operator to get management accounts done and know their sales and margins. In short, don't be a busy fool.

Check the quality of the information you're getting

It's very normal to want to please the boss and so tell him what you think he or she wants to hear. This is not any good for the boss, though, as you need to know the reality of your situation.

A good example of this is when you go into a restaurant and have a meal. It seems to be a matter of course now that your waiter will come and ask you 'Was everything OK with your meal' – in a tone which suggests that anything other than a positive answer will not be welcome.

Yet how often have you not been terribly happy about some aspect of your meal and stayed quiet so as not to make a fuss. If the restaurant was serious about getting feedback from customers, rather than paying lip service to it as part of their approach to customer service, they would ask the question in a way that encouraged you to answer it truthfully.

Probe behind the answers you are given by staff or customers to see what they are really saying. With your staff, assume that they're giving you a truthful answer, but check, just in case – to put your mind at rest.

Continually reassess your business plan as you go along

We get our new business up and running, with the aid of our road map – the business plan. Unfortunately, with all the myriad day-to-day tasks involved in running the business, it's difficult to get back to the business plan and to adjust it in light of the real situation in which your business is now operating, as opposed to the theoretical situation in which you were operating before you started. You know that, six weeks into the new venture, the business plan will be wrong. You'll be doing either worse or better than you thought you would be – but not exactly how you thought you'd be doing.

However you're actually doing, you'll have to adjust your business. For example, your plan will usually have included projections relating to sales and margins. Your sales are easy enough to measure against a budget, but what about your margins? To discover what your margins really are, you're going to have to do at least two stock-takes – and, frankly, they probably don't seem like a priority at this point. Wrong: knowing your actual margins and sales are a key part of your reassessment.

Knowing your sales allows you to figure out what you need to do to lift them. Being aware of your gross margin – which will be different from what you had predicted, and usually worse in the start-up phase – allows you to think about what you can do to change it. Have you a high level of wastage? Is your pricing correct? Is stock being stolen or not run through the till?

If you don't reassess, you probably won't look at your sales or margins until about three months after your first financial year-end, when your accountant forces you to. At that stage, you will have been running your business for fifteen months, most likely not hitting your margin target. In a small- to medium-size business turning over, say, €300,000 per annum, if your gross profit should have been 65 percent but in reality was 55 percent, this will have cost you €30,000 – which I presume you would prefer to have hung on to.

You've got to do whatever it takes (Part II)

There are no excuses when it comes to starting or running a business. There is no one else to pass the buck to; nobody else is responsible for what happens. As nothing ever goes according to plan, are you prepared to do whatever it takes to make sure your venture succeeds?

Once you have an understanding about what is actually happening to you, you must take immediate action to remedy the situation. Letting people go is unpleasant, but it doesn't generally get any easier by being delayed. Changing job roles around, finding the time to do stock-takes, to knock on doors even when you don't want to, to go back, cap in hand, to your bank manager because you are running out of cash are all examples of the type of action you might need to take for your business. None of it is particularly pleasant, but it's part and parcel of the reason you decided to strike out on your own in the first place.

If you only take three things from this chapter . . .

1 Do management accounts every month

2 Be optimistic even when things aren't going well

3 Actively listen to customers, staff and suppliers

Most important of all . . .

Continually reassess your business plan

16

Franchising

Franchising your business for long-term success

In 1993, five years after starting O'Briens, we felt ready to take part in our first franchise exhibition in Dublin. If you're trying to build a franchise network, there are a number of tried-and-tested ways of exposing your business opportunity to prospective franchisees. Along with trade-press advertising, PR and exposure through our existing network of three stores (the Internet had yet to take off as a marketing medium), franchise exhibitions were considered one of the most successful mediums for attracting potential franchisees. Because Ireland is a relatively small market, only one such exhibition is held here each year, so this was an important launch pad for the business.

We had prepared long and hard for our debut in the franchising world. We had almost broken the bank getting our beautiful, glossy, full-colour brochure together and had invested heavily in lawyers' fees, getting our franchise agreements prepared and having our trademarks registered. I had personally written out our first operations manual, presenting O'Briens' business know-how and procedures, so that new franchise partners would know the detail of how to run the business successfully. Most importantly, the retail stores themselves had started to turn the corner and were starting to make some money, so people who were interested in buying an O'Briens franchise could see that they were getting involved with a successful business.

168

Our exhibition stand was a work of art. On a limited budget, we had made it look very professional by dressing it with green-and-white-coloured balloons – our corporate colours; this display had the advantage of being both cheap and visually attractive. I and my assistant Pauline Sexton were decked out in our best bib and tucker. When the doors opened at 10 AM sharp on the first day of the exhibition, I was nervous, but confident that we would be OK.

The actual exhibition surpassed our greatest expectations. We were mobbed. People queued four-deep to get to talk to us. Even though there were only three O'Briens stores open at that time, everybody seemed to know about us. We quickly ran out of brochures and had to send back to the office for more. I was ecstatic: even though I didn't get a break all day, I was on Cloud Nine.

When I eventually got home that evening, tired but very happy, I became quite emotional with Lulu. Here at last was vindication for all the hard work, the sleepless nights, the stress, the financial mess we were only slowly climbing out of. I was almost in tears. I explained to Lulu what had happened that day, how busy we had been, and how we had been the most active exhibitor there. We were on our way at last.

*

Six months later – and it usually takes that long in franchising for an enquiry to develop into an actual sale – I analyzed the results of the exhibition in terms of the number of sales we had made. It was easy to calculate: the number was a single digit – nil, zero, nothing.

These emotional highs and lows characterised our move into franchising, both at home in Ireland, and in the UK. We learnt that everyone at these exhibitions seemed to be a prospective buyer but that, in the cold light of day, when reality set in, they weren't ready for us, or us for them.

On a positive note, our experience at the exhibition injected a sense of pragmatism into our operation which has served us well. Now, when we embark on an exhibition or an advertising campaign, we make a realistic assessment of what we can do rather than a wish-list of what we would like to happen.

I have been involved in franchising for twenty-five years at the time of writing this book, both as a master franchisee (with Prontaprint) and, latterly, as a franchisor. The more time I spend at it, the more I realise how little I really know about it. The advice below comes therefore from a self-confessed amateur who still has much to learn about getting it right.

I was very lucky to have eight years' experience in another franchising company – Prontaprint – before I started O'Briens. Those eight years were tough, but I learnt a lot from them. My experiences at Prontaprint meant that, when it came to starting O'Briens, I had a pretty good idea of how I wanted to do it – or, more importantly, how I *didn't* want to do it. I set myself some simple rules which, I knew through bitter experience, would mean the difference between short-term success and long-term viability for the business.

I have seen many franchise start-ups get things spectacularly wrong after franchising only a couple of units: companies that took on the first person who showed them a chequebook, that thought franchising was a quick-fire way to make big profits, and that tried to franchise their way out of a business that was doomed. In fact, really successful franchising requires a long-term commitment to getting it right, often at the expense of the company's profitability in the early years.

Get the base model right

Almost any business can in theory be franchised successfully, and there are many textbooks and magazines available which cover the diverse range of businesses involved in the franchising. In the UK and Ireland, there are nearly six hundred different franchise systems of various sizes – and that have achieved varying degrees of success. Not all businesses can be franchised, however; there are usually some simple reasons for this:

The cake has to be big enough to be sliced up profitably between the franchisor and the franchisee

In some business models, the margin is not big enough to divide. For example, selling cigarettes, in which the retailer gets a tiny margin, would not lend itself to a franchising model.

The business model has to work, irrespective of whether it's a franchise or not

In other words, the business has to be viable as a business first. Many people have tried franchising to rescue a business format that didn't really work; the unfortunate franchisees who got involved with these companies usually lost everything.

Choose the best franchise partners

It's an old cliché to say that people are the business, but in my experience this is true. One of the bedrocks of the expansion of O'Briens as a franchise business was that, from the beginning, we tried to take into the system only people we thought would make good long-term business partners. It is a truism to say that, in our business, the franchisees that are the most successful and make the most money are inherently successful business people in their own right. Their success is not due to O'Briens but is instead based on the fact that they use the O'Briens franchise system as a tool to create a successful business for themselves. The opposite is also true: many of the small number of our franchisees who are not successful are inherently not good business people in their own right. (And don't believe any company involved in franchising that says it is 100 percent successful.) They might be ideally suited to some other profession – but maybe not running their own business.

At O'Briens, we liken the franchise relationship to a good marriage. Successful marriages are built on a foundation in which, after a wooing process on both sides, each partner gets an opportunity to see the relative strengths and weaknesses of each other, in a truthful and honest way.

Both partners can then go into the relationship with their eyes open, understanding the reality of what they are contemplating – there are few fairy tales in franchising, any more than in marriages – and prepared to act in a mature way to overcome the disputes that will inevitably arise, as they do in any good working relationship.

It was very hard in the early years to reject prospective partners, but I firmly believed that long-term business success could only be built on the back of successful long-term relationships with our customers – our franchisees.

We took our time before entering into any contractual relationship getting to know our new bride or groom. Our first requirement was that, as we were in the hospitality business, we needed 'people persons' to be our partners: the success of our retail stores was based on managing successful relationships with staff and customers. We developed a process of trying out prospective new partners in a real O'Briens store before we would commit to them – or ask them to commit to us. This was a great way of weeding out people who were clearly wrong for our business. These people included the man who refused to work behind the counter in a store because he felt that it was beneath him as a business owner to do so. Then there was the guy who clearly didn't like women, and the woman who turned up late every day and clearly didn't like people of any description, whether they were staff or customers. We had another man who almost got into a fist fight with a customer on the second day of his trial with us. Our attitude was that it was better to find these things out before we got married to them!

McDonalds, which is without doubt the most successful franchisor in the world, despite not getting it right all the time, make it very difficult for prospective franchisees to get into the business. You have to really – and I mean *really* – want to get into McDonalds before they'll take you. They, like us, won't take investor-type franchisees: you have to be prepared to work in the store yourself. Like us, they also realise that the quality of franchisees has a material impact on franchise sales.

Prospective franchisees are attracted to a chain where successful franchisees are already in place. Success breeds success, and like-minded people are attracted to each other. This factor, the 'people factor', will ultimately determine the success or failure of any franchise system in the long term.

Put franchisees' profitability before your own

In the early days, I was, strange as it sounds, delighted to see some of our franchise partners making a lot more money than me. Apart from the pride I took in the fact that they were doing it under our brand, I knew that, in the long term, their success could only be good for the company because the demonstrable success of the concept would help attract bigger and better-quality franchisees into the system.

Too many fledgling franchise companies get this bit wrong and put their profitability before that of their franchisees. Of course, franchisors need to survive while they build up their chain – it's just that this shouldn't be done at the expense of franchisees' profitability.

Love your franchise partners

I want my business associates to know that I would lay down my life for them. I don't mean this literally, but in the sense that I have an absolute commitment and loyalty to them and will do everything I can to help them – and O'Briens – achieve a common goal. I know that many of the people who work with me would do almost anything for me. It's a lovely feeling. And I'm sure that the fact that my colleagues know that I would do almost anything for them makes them feel better about themselves. It's a mutually reinforcing arrangement.

Having that kind of relationship with some of your key franchise partners – and not necessarily the biggest ones – is one of the most powerful forces you could have in a franchise. Of course, it's not possible to have that kind of relationship with a huge number people, and as the chain grows, the percentage of franchisees with whom you can have this type of relationship will fall. Nonetheless, instilling this ethos in your staff, in your corporate culture, and in the way you conduct your business dealings sends an extremely strong message throughout your network.

Earn your royalty

Our job as a franchisor is very simple. It's to grow the sales and profits of our franchisees and, by extension, the brand. If we do this successfully, we will make a good profit. We don't do things the other way round: getting our profits first and then doing a good job delivering sales and profit growth to our franchisees.

Franchisees will generally be content when their businesses are growing, but when the growth stops, even if this is for reasons that are outside your control, they will find reasons to be resentful of the large sums of money they are paying you. It is very important for the franchisor to understand this. We are always dreaming up new ways of improving the business, and we never stop thinking of ways in which we might be able to increase the sales and profitability of our franchisees. Most of our new ideas don't work, and some people think we make a lot of mistakes and are rather accident-prone. But I think you have to be willing to try a lot of different things in order to get a few things to work for you.

The need to impose discipline and not turn into a democracy

This is where the 'iron fist in a velvet glove' quote comes in. No one likes to work in too disciplined an environment. In fact, many of our franchise partners come to us because they have promised themselves that they will never again work for someone else. They want to be their own boss and control their own destiny, not be ordered around any more.

But a brand like O'Briens is built around some clearly defined ideas. For example, we sell good-quality fresh foods in an upmarket Irish-themed environment. Some of our franchisees don't like the colour of our logo; in fact, if they had the chance, they would probably change it. We won't allow that. Some franchisees would like to play the radio as background music, instead of playing Irish music (of which they are free to play whatever type they want). Again, we don't allow it. Others want us to sell chips or french fries alongside sandwiches. Chips or french fries will be sold in O'Briens only over my dead body!

We have had a policy, ever since we started the business, of taking control of all our retail properties. This gave us the ultimate say as to how one of our franchises is run. The downside to this is that, if a store closes for any reason, we are ultimately responsible for the rent. But I think that, as our own money is on the line, we are much more careful about a particular location before we ask a franchise partner to make a big financial commitment to it.

You have to stand up for what you believe in, even if that means attracting the anger of some your franchisees. Some years ago, I tried to introduce some changes to the O'Briens franchise system. These changes involved a significant contractual change, but only for new franchisees who were opening new stores. I didn't think that these changes would disadvantage our franchisees and assumed that the existing franchisees wouldn't have a problem with them. I thought wrong. A small number of franchisees whipped the rest up into a frenzy of moral indignation. I was shocked that the relationships with franchisees that I had carefully nurtured seemed to be falling apart.

I invited the ringleaders of the 'rebellion' in so that we could discuss the situation in a democratic fashion. We would try to arrive at a mutually beneficial compromise. The ringleaders got a sniff of weakness and went for the jugular. For a while, they thought they were running the company, and started to behave in such a way. Demands were made for changes to our existing contracts; these demands had nothing to do with the original dispute. I had made a big mistake; it rattled my confidence, and it took me some years to recover from the hurt and negativity that had been created. It was, however, a good lesson to learn. By all means listen to what your stakeholders have to say – much of it will be sensible and helpful – but bear in mind that franchise businesses do not operate best as democracies. Somebody has to take decisions that are in the interests of everyone.

Imposing discipline in the system is really for the common good. At times, unpopular decisions have to be taken, in the common interest, and strong leadership is required.

Systematize everything

As we developed our business, we wrote down in a series of manuals the right way to do things, and also the way not to do things. This was because I learnt early on that it was inefficient to reinvent the wheel every time we opened a new store and that, by writing things down, we remembered how to do them well. Most importantly, this approach invited accountability. If you train someone how to do a job, give them a manual to back up the training, and they then manage to screw it up, you don't need to have a big argument as to where the fault lies.

In the early days, when we had a problem with the way a franchise partner was operating a store, the franchisee would sometimes claim that they had not been trained in how to carry out a particular function. When we were able to point out to them that we had trained them in that task at their induction-training course, and furthermore could refer to the page in the manual where it was covered, the argument was essentially over. In fact, we coined a term for a franchise partner who asked us questions to which he or she should have known the answer: RTFM, for 'Read the f****** manual'.

Writing things down also meant that, when we started expanding at home and overseas, we had guidelines as to how we should build, open and operate stores. The practice of continually refining how we did things for our Irish market meant that we had ironed out many of the common mistakes we would have made when it came to setting up in a new environment, far from home. Our system of manuals is one of the foundation stones upon which we have built our business.

Understanding the 80:20 rule

Isn't it interesting how the 80:20 rule applies to so many different aspects of life, particularly in business? In franchising, there are lots of uses for it. Like the fact that 80 percent of your profit is likely to come from just 20 percent of your franchise partners, or that, in franchising, you spend 80 percent of your management time dealing with the weakest 20 percent of your operators.

I often think that my job in O'Briens involves letting our very capable management team run the business, while I try to figure out how to deal with the day-to-day crises which are part and parcel of every business, and come up with new ideas to drive us forward. The 'driving us forward' bit is the part that our most profitable franchise partners are interested in, but if we don't put out the fires as we go along, the whole business could potentially go up in flames.

Try to keep your eye on the big picture and not get overwhelmed by problems. The key to O'Briens being successful lies in driving the sales and profits of our franchise partners forward. If we don't spend enough time doing this, the whole business suffers.

Be open to criticism

We at O'Briens never claim to be perfect: although we think we do what we do quite well, we also make mistakes, and almost everything we do could be done better. It's easy for a feeling of arrogance to creep into your business, especially when it's going well.

The dispute with our franchise partners outlined above happened for us at a time when I think I allowed a sense of arrogance to creep into our dealings with our franchise partners. It is understandable that they reacted negatively to it, and some of the changes we proposed should have been thought through better. But my reaction was to become defensive and deny that anything was wrong. That was a mistake.

Help your weakest members get up to speed

It is a fact of business life that each franchisee's business will develop at a different pace, despite the fact that they are all trading under a common format. Most new businesses get off to a reasonable start in O'Briens, but about one in ten struggle to break into profitability at the beginning. These businesses need special attention if they are to turn the corner and become successful. For these cases, we first try to find the root cause of the problem and then, if we can, do something about it.

Celebrate and recognise achievement

We love parties in O'Briens and, if I say so myself, it's something we do rather well. We relish an opportunity to express ourselves (or show off!) and bring everyone involved in running the business together to celebrate our unique relationship. This includes all our suppliers and service providers, through to our staff and franchise partners.

Every year in January, we hold our annual conference and Feis Mór ('Big Party'). We start preparing for it the week after the last one ended. Three months before it happens, we move into high gear. Every last detail of the conference and the Feis Mór are planned down to the tiniest detail. Everything must be perfect on the day; nothing can be left to chance.

As the conference week approaches, everyone in O'Briens becomes involved. Tension runs high, nerves are stretched, the core team puts in long hours. Last-minute hitches are dealt with, and the show is on!

Our conferences also give us a great opportunity to recognise publicly the success of all the stakeholders in our enterprise. From our partners who have had a really tough year to our most blasé success stories, and from our own support team to our long-serving – and long-suffering – suppliers, we all love acknowledgement that we're doing well in some aspect of our businesses. For many of those who attend our conference, this is the first time they have been up on a stage to receive a token of thanks for the sweat and blood they have shed in the year just past.

Recognition, of course, doesn't have to be confined to big set pieces like conferences. It can be as simple as saying 'thank you'. I don't believe you can say it often enough. I make a conscious effort to say thank you to people in the O'Briens organisation as often as I can during the day.

At smaller regional meetings, and when visiting stores, where you get to meet the staff, there's always a chance to make somebody feel better about themselves. This creates the all-important feel-good factor.

Franchising overseas

In early 1997, I received a telephone call at my office in Dublin. O'Briens was beginning to find its feet as a business. We were up to about twenty outlets, with the first few opened in the UK, spearheading our expansion in that market.

On the phone was a man called Hugh Hoyes-Cock. He wanted to come and see me to discuss setting up a master franchise for O'Briens in Singapore. I wasn't entirely sure where Singapore was!

Hugh had an interesting story. A British accountant, he had been living in Singapore for the last twenty years, working for large multinational companies. His son Alex was attending the Royal College of Surgeons in Dublin, studying to be a doctor. Alex had written to his Dad about this great sandwich bar in Dublin called O'Briens, where he got his lunch every day. On Hugh's next visit to Dublin to visit Alex, he called in to see for himself what the store was like.

It was after that visit that I got the phone call. Some months later, we entered into a master-franchise agreement for eleven countries in Asia. Just as we were about to sign the agreement, Hugh said to me: 'What about Laos and Cambodia?' 'Go on then,' I said, 'you can have them' – and thus I 'gave away' two sovereign countries for nothing!

Our master franchise in Asia was the first of a string of such franchises we have developed around the world. Notwithstanding the fact that we knew nothing about the market in Singapore, it made sense for us to develop in this way, for three main reasons:

The right person in the right place

While we knew nothing about Singapore, Hugh did. From the best locations to set up a sandwich-bar business, to where to buy vegetables and meat, to understanding the marketing mediums, Hugh brought his local knowledge, and his personal drive and enthusiasm, to the project – and therefore made it possible.

The concept was already properly developed

As we had been systematising and recording how the business worked for a long time before Hugh came along, it was no problem to let him share in the work we had already done. We packed our shop-fitting manual and our marketing and operations manuals into a box, gave Hugh an intensive three-week training course, and sent him back to Singapore to get on with it – which, to his credit, he did.

When we looked, the markets were actually similar

Not knowing much about it, at first glance we assumed that Singapore was very different from Ireland or Britain. People I talked to about the proposed move were sceptical, however. 'Asians don't eat bread – their staple diet is rice and noodles' was a typical comment – and, superficially at least, it seemed to ring true.

In Ireland or Britain, our typical customer is a young, white-collar female, with a high disposable income, who takes a lunch hour, eats food based around bread and coffee, wears Levis and listens to U2. When we took a serious look at the market for our products in downtown Singapore, we found that it was identical to what we had in Dublin. Incidentally, we have found the same typical customer base for our products in almost every market in which we operate around the world.

As we have expanded abroad, I have learnt to look for the similarities between the various markets rather than the differences – which are a reason *not* to do something. Underneath it all, we have much more in common, as citizens of the world, than we commonly acknowledge.

If you only take three things from this chapter . . .

1   Get the base model for the franchise right

2   Choose a franchise partner as you would a life partner

3   Put franchisees' profitability before your own

Most important of all . . .

Earn your royalty

17

Being Good Is Good Business

Why being responsible in your community gives you an edge

We discovered rather late in the evolution of our business that involving the business in a charitable effort was not just good in terms of publicity but, far more significantly, made the stakeholders in the business – staff, suppliers and customers – feel better about their relationship with the company. In fact, it had such a good effect that we have made it one of our corporate goals to adopt an appropriate cause and devote management time to helping others, just as we manage all the other aspects of the business. We took this approach to our involvement with the Special Olympics World Summer Games, which took place in Ireland in 2003.

We got involved in the Games partly because I had an interest in people with learning disabilities but, to be honest, also because we could see that there was a significant commercial benefit in having our small brand name elevated to the big time by its association with a large, prestigious event. What we hadn't expected was the goodwill and team spirit the Games engendered for all the people associated with us. Our people really felt better about themselves and the company; as a result, productivity improved, staff felt more loyal to the company, customers who might have drifted away stayed with us, and a great feeling was created throughout the business.

What follows is the story of our first involvement with what is fashionably known as 'corporate social responsibility'.

*

It was a bright, sunny morning in Anchorage, as a polite American soldier drove us across town to the venue where the skiing events were being held. There was a lot more snow in Alaska than we were used to in Ireland, and it was banked up in dirty mounds along the edge of the road. As we exited the town and headed for the mountains, Lulu and I looked forward to the day with some trepidation. We were on our way to see the Irish downhill-skiing team compete in the Special Olympics World Winter Games, as guests of the Irish organisers, as a prelude to the World Summer Games, which were to be held in Ireland in the summer of 2003.

We were nervous because this was to be our first real exposure to the Special Olympics people: the athletes, coaches, family members, supporters and organisers of one kind or another. Our exposure to people with learning disabilities up till then had been virtually nil, apart from some immediate relatives, and I was frankly scared about my first encounter with such people.

That day changed our lives for the better. Throughout the day, and for the rest of the trip, we walked around with lumps in our throats as we observed the triumphs and tragedies experienced by – and the love and emotion shown by – all the people on the slopes. Not given to overt displays of emotion, I found myself crying quietly to myself.

The Irish team performed magnificently for their country, notwithstanding that, for a number of athletes, this was their first time skiing on real snow! At the awards ceremonies for the hockey event that evening, we saw the Special Olympics schools-enrichment programme in action. The team from Brazil was being supported by a school from a remote town in Alaska. The children had made Brazilian flags, bunting and posters, and had roared and screamed their way through the match, in support of 'their' team. When they finally won, all the schoolkids went crazy and came down to the edge of the playing area and got the athletes to sign autographs for them. Here was the normal stereotype about people with learning disabilities being turned on its head. Here the athletes were the kings, and boy did they know it. It was incredibly emotional. We were all profoundly touched: the Games brought out the best in people. I wanted to be part of it: I knew that we had made a good decision in getting involved in the Special Olympics and that our sponsorship of the Summer Games in Ireland was going to work.

*

It must have been around April 2000. I was watching a documentary one evening on TV about the Special Olympics World Summer Games, which had been held in North Carolina, USA, in 1999. The documentary was being shown because it had just been announced that Ireland had been awarded the Games for the summer of 2003. A couple of years prior to this, one of my godchildren, Daniel, had been born with Down's syndrome. I also have another godson, Philip, who lives in Canada, who has a learning disability. I was interested in the subject because it was now part of my life.

I realised that the project was likely to have a huge impact in a small country like Ireland, and I felt that we could use our stores to publicise the event, raise money, or whatever. It didn't escape me either that this project could also put a small company like O'Briens on the map.

The next day, I contacted the chairman of the organising committee, Denis O'Brien, offering our services. He told me later that I was the first person who had contacted him after the programme – which goes to show that the early bird catches the worm. Some months later, we signed up as one of the official sponsors, agreeing to donate the not-insignificant sum of €1.27 million, partly in cash and partly by feeding the athletes and volunteers during the Games themselves. We also lent our weight to the volunteer programme in particular: each of the main sponsors got to work with a paricular aspect of the Games management. There was no question of writing a cheque for €1.27 million: we didn't have that kind of money. But we did feel that, by being properly organised, leveraging our goodwill, and putting in a team effort, we could come up with the loot. I have no doubt that it was one of the best commercial decisions I ever took for O'Briens.

The Special Olympics is a sporting movement for people with learning disabilities. The movement is about inclusion, not exclusion, and about the athletes reaching their potential, not about trying to make them into something they're not. Each year national games are held, in the different countries, and every four years, there is a World Games. The Irish Games were the first time the event had been held outside the United States. It was to be the biggest sporting event in the world in 2003.

Learning disability is one of those things that everybody's aware of but that nobody outside those immediately involved talks about much. I realised that most people in the country must be touched by learning disability in some way. Everyone has a family member, relation or friend who either has to deal with this subject or knows someone who does. As we got more involved with the Special Olympics, I became aware of the enormous amount of good that was being done by the parents, coaches and general volunteers who were working with the athletes. Most of the time they had a very hard job, with little public recognition. For the parents in particular, it was a life sentence; I use the expression guardedly. Whereas, in the normal course of events, you expect to rear your children and then see them move on, this will not be the experience of many people who have a child with a learning difficulty. Their child is likely to be with them until the parents die; there is no retirement. And there is also the problem for the parent of worrying about who will look after the child when they pass on. Despite this, the positive attitudes displayed by all these people really inspired me. It certainly put my own life – and those of most people – in perspective.

As is often the case, I bit off more than I could chew. Committing to provide €1.27 million was the easy bit. As we didn't have anything like that kind of money available, we agreed with the organisers that we would fund-raise for it. I persuaded my mother-in-law, Alyne Healy, who had experience of running the Irish Migraine Association, to head up our Special Olympics project, and we spent the first six months after we had made the commitment planning what we would do – in terms of getting the money and, just as importantly, figuring out how we would feed everyone.

I was really touched by the way in which my friends and business colleagues rallied around the cause. I know that, at the beginning, most of them didn't really understand what they were getting involved in. Lulu and I had been to Alaska, and we knew how life-changing being involved in the Games could be, but I didn't think we could explain it to other people.

We organised and ran some big events. A cycle from Dublin to my beloved Sligo, in which a number of our franchise partners took part. A white-tie ball. (I will never get involved in organising a ball again; I virtually prostituted myself to sell tables.) A 'Golf Classic' which Padraig Harrington, one of the world's top golfers, attended. I don't play golf. I don't like Pringle sweaters or turtle-neck jumpers. I was very sceptical about how much could be raised from such an event. Fiacra Nagle, my friend and O'Briens' Irish managing director, who organised it, got some cynical support from me. He raised €250,000 from the event. I was silenced.

We had an art auction in the RHA, Dublin's top art venue. We built the world's tallest sandwich in Cork. We launched our new soft-drink range by charging an extra ten cent on every bottle; each ten cent went to the fund. Maria Doyle Kennedy and Sinead O'Connor headlined a concert with the cream of Irish contemporary musicians at Dublin's Olympia Theatre.

On a smaller scale, friends, family members and work colleagues took part in the women's mini-marathon in Dublin. There was a money-box scheme, where we placed boxes in our own stores as well as in those of other friendly retailers. Our kids and the neighbours' kids raised €53 by staging a play for their parents. Lulu and her colleagues organised a drink-till-you-drop evening. (The less said about that the better!) My sister Caroline organised a casino night, my sister-in-law Anna a sponsored walk. There was a fashion show in Cork, a photography competition, a cycle to John o'Groats, and a walk around the Highland Way in Scotland. It all became very time-consuming, but we made it in the end.

The Games themselves took place in June 2003. I felt that we had maxed out on our sponsorship already, in that we had received excellent media exposure for our involvement with the Games over the previous two years. People associated us strongly with the Games, sometimes thinking that we were the main sponsor, rather than, as was actually the case, one of six secondary sponsors after Bank of Ireland. I had overlooked the impact the Games themselves would have.

The opening ceremony took place in Croke Park, Ireland's largest, most modern stadium. We had allocated tickets on the basis of who had helped most with our fund-raising and catering efforts. I remember standing in the crowd, before the ceremony started, noticing that there was no advertising visible in the stadium. You might think that, as one of the main sponsors, we would object to this, but I didn't: it was entirely appropriate for the occasion. Anyway, there were thousands of volunteers milling around dressed in uniforms that featured our logo: the exposure for O'Briens was superb. There were rumblings from some of the other sponsors, but there was nothing they could do about it.

It was apparent from the off that the Special Olympics would be really special. There was a fantastic atmosphere, and the stadium looked magnificent. All the spectators had been given coloured flags, and the parade of athletes from the various countries was very moving. Celebrities like Muhammad Ali and Arnold Schwarzenegger accompanied the teams as they entered the stadium. The team from the UK got a great cheer. I had to draw breath: a team from the UK getting a huge cheer as they entered Croke Park? You would have to be Irish to understand the significance of that!

The entertainment was outstanding: from the world's largest Riverdance line to Bono from U2 introducing Nelson Mandela, while their anthem 'Pride' played in the background. There was a group of VIPs sitting just in front of us. At the beginning, they had left their flags beside their seats, their body language saying: 'We don't do flags, we're VIPs.' Halfway through the ceremony, I noticed that they were waving them half-heartedly; by the end of the evening, they were waving them furiously and singing along to the songs, just like the rest of us.

The culmination of the ceremony was the lighting of the Olympic flame. Special Olympics athletes, accompanied by police officers from the PSNI and the Gardaí on motorbikes, carried it on the final stage of its journey from Greece. A final wave of emotion gripped the crowd as the flame reached the stage. People around us were openly crying and hugging each other. I felt so proud to be Irish, and so proud of the part that O'Briens had played in the proceedings.

During the Games themselves, I spent the week visiting the venues, thanking the catering staff who were flying the flag for O'Briens. The volunteers were genuinely touched by their experience: many of them told me that it was the best experience of their lives, and they meant it. People were working together in a way they hadn't done before. There was no bitching, and I heard no complaints about our sandwiches. I know that there must have been some – after all, we were supplying twenty thousand a day during the Games – but we didn't hear any.

A lot of business people, myself included, tend to write off the voluntary sector, but this was a superbly organised week, on a par with anything I have ever been part of. The athletes themselves swept all before them. It helped change people's attitudes towards people with learning disabilities.

Overall, O'Briens' involvement in the 2003 Special Olympics was a really rewarding experience. Our staff, franchise partners, suppliers and customers all bought into it in varying degrees. It provided a focus for our team-building efforts, as we collectively rallied around a common cause. I know that our staff, and all the people we came into contact with, liked the fact that we were involved in it. There's still a feel-good factor in the air. It brought out the best in our people, and O'Briens as a company has done something really worthwhile.

*

Here are some things to think about as you wake up to the possibilities that being good in business bring:

You don't have to be a big company to do something

No matter what size your business, you can do something locally to create a point of difference compared with your competitors and, more importantly, 'switch on' the people who are associated with your enterprise. Being good is a genuine win-win situation for you. You do something good and you get substantially more back in return for your efforts.

Find something you're passionate about

Have you ever witnessed something that has moved you, or been touched by some organisation's kindness or involvement in the community? Or has a particular organisation helped someone who is close to you, or made life bearable for others? Could your company 'adopt' that organisation, or could you partner with them to achieve a specific goal?

Be part of your community

Find something that will have significance for your staff and customers and, just as important, that relates to your business. A local hurling team, a van for a day-care centre, litter bins in the town centre, trees in the park, the flower club. It doesn't matter whether your efforts amount to hundreds of euro, or thousands

– the point is that you are doing something for reasons other than direct commercial gain. People, especially your customers, will like that.

Make sure you're doing it for the right reasons, not as a cynical exercise

While your staff and customers will applaud you for making the right decision, they will see through a cynical effort which is deemed to be exploitative or inappropriate. If you really aren't passionate about helping others in some way, maybe it would be better not to bother.

Commit to a goal, plan and execute

As with any other aspect of your business, you need to make a commitment of people and resources, set goals for what you want to achieve from your efforts, and then execute the plan. One of the things that works very well for us is bringing in a retired person who acts as our charity co-ordinator on a part time basis. This means that somebody keeps an eye on your 'being good' bit while you concentrate on the 'commercial' bit of your business. We get an extra benefit from having an older person in the business: their wise eyes and ears make the company a better place to work for the whole staff.

If you only take three things from this chapter . . .

1 Even small companies can do something to benefit the local community

2 Find something you're passionate about

3 Commit enough people and resources to the project

Most important of all . . .

Make sure you're doing it for the right reasons

Conclusion

There are times over the years when I've said to myself: 'There's no way I would ever do this again. The pain and grief I suffered ruined some of my early years', but you know, this feeling never lasts long, and I honestly feel that I have lived my life, so far, to the full, and that's the important thing for me. It has been a very rewarding experience for Lulu and me as we have made our lives together. We have gone through low lows: dark times when nothing was going well for us. But when things did start going right, the good times were all the sweeter, and we appreciated them.

Starting a business, or indeed taking over one, involves risk – to your financial well-being and to your pride – because, if it goes pear-shaped, there's usually no one else to blame. We take this risk for a reason, though. To be able to look back and say: 'I made that; I have made a difference.' To achieve the financial goals you have set for yourself is a marvellously liberating experience. Having the respect of your peers and the freedom to pursue what you would like to do, as opposed to what you *have* to do, is very satisfying.

Running a business isn't for everyone. That doesn't stop many of us dreaming about it, though. Recognising your own situation – your need for security and certainty, for example – can help you rationalise a difficult decision.

Some readers may have been put off by what they read in this book. Their illusions about what running a business means may have been shattered. On the other hand, you may have been excited by what you read and recognised yourself in some of the examples I have given.

Whatever the case may be, the objective of this book has been to give a realistic description of what setting up and running a business is like. I wanted you to feel challenged by its contents rather than being fed the cosy fairy tales that a lot of business books seem to promote.

If you haven't got it yet, understand that it's all about you, the owner/manager. Every other aspect of setting up and running a business is subservient to this inescapable reality.

If you're serious about starting a business and you have thought it through, I would just go for it. There's never a 'right' time to do it, and you'll go old and grey while you wait for it to come along. Life is for living, and living involves risk-taking. But isn't it better to have tried than to have regrets about what you didn't do when you were young enough and had the energy?

Finally, if you're going to put all this blood, sweat and tears into it, make it worth your while. Good luck and bon voyage!